T0069516

BEETHOVEN

BEETHOVEN

BEETHOVEN

Variations on a Life

Mark Evan Bonds

OXFORD
UNIVERSITY PRESS

OXFORD
UNIVERSITY PRESS

Oxford University Press is a department of the University of Oxford. It furthers
the University's objective of excellence in research, scholarship, and education
by publishing worldwide. Oxford is a registered trade mark of Oxford University
Press in the UK and certain other countries.

Published in the United States of America by Oxford University Press
198 Madison Avenue, New York, NY 10016, United States of America.

Library of Congress Cataloging-in-Publication Data
Names: Bonds, Mark Evan, author.
Title: Beethoven : variations on a life / Mark Evan Bonds.
Description: New York : Oxford University Press, 2020. |
Includes bibliographical references and index.
Identifiers: LCCN 2019053066 (print) | LCCN 2019053067 (ebook) |
ISBN 9780190054083 (hardback) | ISBN 9780190054106 (epub)
Subjects: LCSH: Beethoven, Ludwig van, 1770–1827. |
Composers—Germany—Biography. |
Composer—Austria—Biography.
Classification: LCC ML410.B4 B58 2020 (print) | LCC ML410.B4 (ebook) |
DDC 780.92 [B]—dc23
LC record available at https://lccn.loc.gov/2019053066
LC ebook record available at https://lccn.loc.gov/2019053067

3 5 7 9 8 6 4 2

Printed by Sheridan Books, Inc., United States of America

To Michael Morse

CONTENTS

ACKNOWLEDGMENTS

I am grateful to Tim Carter, Annegret Fauser, and Stefan Litwin, my colleagues at the University of North Carolina at Chapel Hill, for their spirited feedback throughout the process of writing this book. I owe thanks as well to Robert Bonds, Tom McAuley, Michael Morse, Massimo Ossi, James Parsons, Gilbert Sewall, John D. Wilson, and Jeremy Yudkin for their insightful comments on various earlier versions of the text. Sam Hammond provided his typically keen critical eye, generous spirit, and the index. Nancy Toff, my editor at Oxford University Press, gave expert guidance from start to finish.

Dorothea, Peter, and Andrew were there in all ways once again. Thank you.

Introduction

Vienna, March 26, 1827, late afternoon. Having scrawled his name to a legal document with the little strength he has left, the gravely ill and nearly deaf composer is now in a coma. A bolt of lightning splits the sky. A clap of thunder follows. Beethoven opens his eyes, raises a fist toward heaven, sinks back, and dies.

So legend would have it. Or at least one of the legends. Accounts of Beethoven's death vary widely, and this one dates from more than thirty years after the event.[1] There may be a grain of truth to it, for weather records confirm the early spring thunderstorm that day, even if other details remain suspect. Separating fact from fiction is a major challenge for anyone who wants to come to grips with Beethoven and his music.

Yet even without the fiction, Beethoven's life is the stuff of movies. The characters and the plot are ready-made for the screen: a talented young musician, the son of an alcoholic father, leaves his provincial home and dazzles high society in the imperial capital as a pianist and composer. But tragedy strikes in the form of deafness, and our hero, rejected by the woman he loves, withdraws into a world of his own and writes music he cannot hear. He turns his isolation into an asset and wins acclaim as his generation's greatest composer of instrumental music. Commissions from abroad pour in during the final years of his life. Tens of thousands attend his funeral.

It is a compelling story and true enough in its outlines. But where does the music fit into all this? Generations of critics—including Hollywood scriptwriters—have projected Beethoven's life onto his works, treating his music as if it were the soundtrack to the life. The temptation is understandable, for his style did indeed change markedly over the course of his career. If we know anything about his life at all, it is difficult to hear the unconventional piano sonatas and string quartets of his last decade without imagining the sense of isolation his near-total deafness must have forced on him. When we listen to these late compositions against the backdrop of those earlier works from the "heroic" period—works that, like the Fifth Symphony, move from struggle to triumph—we sense that something has changed in the person who created them.

The temptation to map the works onto the life is particularly strong in biographies, which by their very nature move in a more or less straight line through time, with the music often functioning as an audible diary of sorts. But this chronological approach, valuable as it may be, creates its share of blind spots. It tends to emphasize change over continuity and favor those works that move the stylistic needle toward a destination we know in advance. It struggles to account for large swaths of the composer's output and downplays those many compositions that do not fit the narrative of continuous change.

Beethoven: Variations on a Life is not a biography, nor does it follow a chronological path. For all the ups and downs of his personal life and professional career, Beethoven remained remarkably consistent in his most fundamental convictions about himself and his art, and it is this inner consistency that provides the key to understanding the relationship between his life and his works. Beethoven approached music in much the same way he approached life. He liked to adopt multiple perspectives on whatever attracted his attention: a thematic idea, a musical genre, a friend, a patron, money, politics, religion. He did not go through life with a perpetual frown on his face, and we should be wary of equating too quickly the emotions we hear in his music with his own personal feelings. Indeed, we shortchange our experience of his music if we think of him as the misanthropic, suffering soul he has so often been made out to be. His music is the creation of an individual far more complex than the iconic scowl.

The question, then, is not how any particular event shaped any particular work, but rather how the events of his life shaped his broader vision of his art, which ultimately served to frame everything he wrote. The life, in other words, influenced the works, though not in ways that allow us to draw direct lines between the two. The challenge is to relate Beethoven to all of his music and not to just some of it. This means going beyond the triumphant "heroic" compositions to include such works as the zany Eighth Symphony, the enigmatic Bagatelle for piano, op. 126, no. 1, and the Janus-faced finale of the "Serioso" String Quartet, op. 95.

Beethoven thought of himself not simply as a composer but as a "tone-poet" (*Tondichter*), an artist who poeticizes through music. This was, in his time, a new word for a new kind of artist. And it is particularly fitting in Beethoven's case, for his music, like poetry, speaks to something deep within the human soul and demands interpretation. It compels us to move beyond the immediacy of the surface to grasp what it is that stirs us so profoundly. "Tone-poet" remains as timely today, some 250 years after Beethoven's birth, as it was during his own lifetime.

Chapter 1

The Scowl

There are no right or wrong ways to listen to Beethoven's music, but some are more accommodating than others. The first thing to get past is The Scowl. It is hard to avoid, for it confronts us everywhere, from album covers and dust jackets to monumental statues and those little white busts that adorn upright pianos. Even experienced listeners find it difficult to repress the stern visage behind the music. When we hear works such as the Fifth Symphony or the "Appassionata" Sonata that are intense and even violent, it fits. And we can be forgiven if we conjure up the image of a deeply furrowed brow when we listen to the gloomy, meditative first movement of the "Moonlight" Sonata. The Scowl is an outward manifestation of inner turmoil, and these are the kinds of works that seem to come directly from the soul of their creator.

Yet when we listen to works that contradict this rictus of suffering—the laugh-out-loud Eighth Symphony or the tuneful, rollicking finale of the Piano Sonata, op. 79, for example—we struggle to reconcile what we are hearing with the image of a composer who was supposedly self-absorbed, turned inward, and uninterested in presenting himself to the world in any sort of agreeable manner. We are disappointed, moreover, by the very existence of such crowd-pleasing potboilers as *Wellington's Victory*, complete with simulated cannon- and musket-fire, or *Der glorreiche Augenblick* ("The Glorious Moment"), written for the Congress of Vienna in 1814 to celebrate the restoration of monarchical rule across Europe in the wake of Napoleon. For many listeners, such works somehow do not represent the "real" Beethoven, that is, the scowling Beethoven.

What, then, are we to do with all those many works—the bulk of his output, in fact—that contradict The Scowl? One option is to listen to Beethoven in the way his contemporaries did. This involves more than playing his music on period instruments and attending to performance practices of his time. Our ears could benefit from a change, too. We cannot erase from our minds all the music we know from the past two centuries, but we can approach his works with fresh ears if we try to put ourselves in the concert-hall seats of Beethoven's contemporaries.

To begin with, they had no notion of The Scowl. The average music-lover of Beethoven's day knew very little about him as a person. The few images of him that circulated during his lifetime show a serious face, but this was true of almost any formal portrait of that era. The Scowl became iconic only later, reinforced by such turbulent (and popular) works as the "Pathétique," "Moonlight," and "Appassionata" piano sonatas, and above all the Fifth Symphony. In his own time, "Beethoven" was little more than a name. Even E. T. A. Hoffmann (of "Nutcracker" fame), who in the 1810s wrote lengthy and penetrating critiques of the composer's works, seems to have known next to nothing about the person behind the music. Nor did the composer's contemporaries know much about his deafness, especially if they lived outside of Vienna. The earliest published account of it appeared in 1816, and only toward the end of his life did critics began to speculate on how this condition might have been affecting his latest works.[1] Not until after his death did the circumstance of deafness become central to the perception of his music.

Even when the performers smile, the composer scowls. The conductor Vasily Petrenko gestures toward a bust of Beethoven after a 2013 Proms concert at the Royal Albert Hall, London. Created by Johann Nepomuk Schaller sometime after 1827, the bust regularly adorned the stage of Royal Philharmonic Society concerts from 1871 until the 1980s. *BBC Proms*

What is more revealing still is that even those in Vienna who were aware of his deafness, his unhappy love affairs, and his generally dour public countenance did not hear his music as an expression of his inner self. The reason for this was quite simple: they did not hear anyone's music in this way. It would not have occurred to even the most sophisticated listeners of the time to hear music as a form of sonic autobiography. Audiences judged what they heard on its ability to move them. The notion that the emotions portrayed in a sonata or symphony might be those of the composer would have been quite foreign to Beethoven's contemporaries. Literature was another matter: there, the idea of autobiographical art had taken hold more than a generation before, and Goethe was one of its chief proponents, at least in his early years. His works, he declared in his autobiography, were "fragments of a great confession," and readers absorbed them as such.[2]

Music, however, was slow to catch up. Listeners began to hear Beethoven's works as self-expressive only in retrospect. When the first biographies began to appear, shortly after his death, audiences learned for the first time of the composer's constant ill-health, and they began to hear the third movement of the String Quartet in A minor, op. 132, labeled "A Convalescent's Holy Song of Thanksgiving to the Deity," as Beethoven's own personal song of thanksgiving. When they read about his profound love of nature, they began to hear the "Pastoral" Symphony as an expression of *his* love of nature. When they read in his correspondence of his resolve to "grab fate by the throat," they heard the Fifth Symphony as a musical expression of that resolve.

It soon became an article of faith that Beethoven had bared his soul in his music. The French critic Chrétien Urhan deemed the Ninth Symphony a summary of its creator's "entire life," the "secret of his entire inner existence," his "moral biography," and the Russian biographer Alexandre Oulibicheff declared that what he sought in the composer's music was "above all Beethoven himself, the innermost of his self."[3] "With Beethoven's symphonies," the German critic and literary historian Julian Schmidt observed in 1853, "we have the feeling that we are dealing with something very different from the usual alternations of joy and sorrow in which wordless music ordinarily moves. We intuit the mysterious abyss of a spiritual world, and we torment ourselves in an effort to understand it. . . . We want to know what drove the tone-poet to bottomless despair and to unalloyed joy; we want to gain an understanding from the mysteriously beautiful features of this sphinx."[4]

But all this lay in the future. Listeners in Beethoven's own lifetime regarded him more in the manner of Shakespeare, a figure about whom they knew even less but whom they admired all the more as an author of immense emotional and technical range, an author capable of transcending any one particular genre or mood. Readers marveled in particular at Shakespeare's ability to juxtapose not only contrasting and diverse characters in a single work (Iago and Desdemona, Lear and Cordelia, Shylock and Portia) but also contrasting and diverse modes of drama. The shift from tragic to comic and back again occurs with stunning frequency in his plays, and they heard the same sort of contrast in Beethoven's music. It is scarcely coincidental that the composer's contemporaries likened him to Shakespeare on more than one occasion, or that he himself was a devoted enthusiast of the Bard.

As we listen, then, it helps to remember that Beethoven's audiences regarded all composers rather as playwrights, musical scores as the equivalent of scripts, performers as actors. And they valued the variety that came with such emotional elasticity. When a Viennese critic of the time called Beethoven "our Proteus," he did so with pride and respect, for like the shape-shifting sea-god, only the Protean artist had the ability to take on whatever form he chose. Such an artist could transcend the limits of self-inclination and embrace any imaginable emotion or state of mind.[5] "To be truly free and educated," as the poet and philosopher Friedrich Schlegel noted at the time, "an individual would have to be able to tune himself at will and at any time philosophically or philologically, critically or poetically, historically or rhetorically, à l'antique or à la moderne, in an entirely arbitrary fashion and to any degree, in the way one tunes an instrument."[6]

Beethoven in 1818, sketch by August von Kloeber. The gaze is contemplative, not scowling. *Universal History Archive/UIG/Shutterstock*

By this line of thought, Beethoven tuned and retuned himself constantly. He was nothing if not Protean, consistently capable of assuming new guises in his art. He adopted a certain sense of distance while composing. As Hoffmann put it in his 1810 review of the Fifth Symphony, Beethoven "separates his 'I' from the inner realm of musical tones and commands that domain as an absolute ruler."[7] Beethoven could and no doubt did use music as an outlet for his personal feelings on more than one occasion, but to assume that this was his standard way of composing leads to a rather narrow mode of perception, one in which we welcome those works that correspond to The Scowl and marginalize those that do not.

The astonishing variety of Beethoven's music compels us to look elsewhere for a common creative denominator. Paradoxical as it may seem, Beethoven's ability to adopt multiple perspectives toward any given object was a constant feature of his inner self. He approached music in much the same way he approached everything in life. He liked to look at whatever was before him—a musical idea, a name, a word, a poem, a social situation, even another person—from many different angles and explore their implications and consequences to the fullest.

The best-known example of this in his music is the four-note opening of the Fifth Symphony. The motif (with its distinctive rhythm of short-short-short-LONG) returns repeatedly throughout all four movements but never in exactly the same form. Beethoven changes its pitches, intervals, harmony, and instrumentation, and at times retains only the rhythm. Having presented the idea in unison at the very beginning of the first movement, he proceeds at once to manipulate it: the first violins, second violins, and violas toss the brief fragment around among themselves, almost as if they were playing a game of tag, changing the pitches slightly each time. The other instruments of the orchestra soon join in, and we hear at once how malleable this brief and seemingly simple musical idea really is. Even when Beethoven introduces a contrasting lyrical theme—marked *dolce* ("sweetly")—we hear a variant of the four-note motif rumbling along underneath in the low strings.

This sort of intense thematic manipulation is basic to almost everything Beethoven wrote. He liked the challenge of making something out of almost nothing, and better still, making many somethings out of a single almost-nothing. The greater the contrast the better. The opening of the Piano Trio in D Major, op. 70, no. 1 ("Ghost") begins with a loud, almost violent downward four-note unison gesture that is repeated in rapid succession by all three instruments playing in unison, each time starting on an ever-higher note. The idea could scarcely be simpler. But after the fifth time, the cello, without warning, inverts this downward figure and turns it into the beginning of a lyrical melody that soars upward and then goes on to serve as the principal theme for the movement as a whole. Whether we realize it or not, these two very different themes reveal different perspectives on a single basic idea. The sketchbooks bear repeated witness to thematic manipulations of this kind. Once he had alighted upon a musical idea, no matter how brief, Beethoven would jot it down and begin to explore its potential by looking at it from multiple perspectives.

Beethoven treated language in much the same way. At the beginning of the finale to his last string quartet, op. 135, he added words beneath the movement's two principal motifs. The cello opens by asking, *Muss es sein?* ("Must it be?"), the words set to a simple three-note motif that moves down and then up, in a contour that mirrors a questioning tone of voice. The words are not meant to be sung, though the three syllables fit the notes precisely. The tempo is slow, the mode is minor, the mood somber. This darkness disappears the moment the tempo shifts from slow to fast and the mode from minor to major. Here, the motif moves up and then down, emulating the contour of a declarative statement, for it is at this point that Beethoven provides the answer to the question by inverting the order of the opening two syllables: *Es muss sein!* ("It must be!"). Exactly what "it" is has long been a matter of speculation. Beethoven labeled the whole movement "The Resolution Achieved with Difficulty," but the object of that resolution has elicited widely varying explanations extending from the trivial (the composer's response to his cook's request for more money) to the metaphysical (a joyous acceptance of mortality). This in itself points to the ability of the music to take us in multiple different directions at the same time. Like words, notes are capable of manipulations that can change their meanings entirely.

Beethoven's correspondence is full of such verbal permutations. He once closed a letter to his friend Nicholas von Zmeskall, who happened to be a baron, with this curious string of variations:

adieu Baron Ba . . . ron ron / nor / orn / rno / onr

and glossed it with a mixture of French and German: "*Voilà quelque chose* aus dem alten versazAmt" ("There is something from the old pawnshop"), punning on the German word *Versatzamt* (pawnshop), itself based on the root word *versetzen* (to "transpose"), in the sense not only of goods exchanged for money (as in a pawnshop) but also in the sense of letters—movable type—that have been transposed, hence the five different possible permutations on the last three letters of "Baron."[8]

Beethoven could never resist a good pun. He enjoyed playing on the similar sounds of words like *gelehrt* (learned) and *geleert* (emptied), *Verleger* (publisher) and *verlegen* (embarrassed), *Not* (need) and *Note* (musical note). These, too, are verbal manifestations of what Beethoven liked to do with musical themes: turn them inside out and upside down to make the same basic material function in very different ways. Musical puns abound in his music. The loud opening phrase of the first movement of the Eighth Symphony, for example, functions as its quiet final cadence: what we remember as the opening of the movement also turns out to be its close. Beethoven was not the first to do this kind of thing: Joseph Haydn had led the way a generation before. But Beethoven took this tendency to a new extreme, so much so that he managed to baffle even many of his contemporaries who *wanted* to understand his music.

The ability to look at a single object from multiple perspectives is delightfully evident in his two different settings of "L'amante impaziente" ("The Impatient Lover"), op. 82, nos. 3 and 4, for solo voice and piano. The text is an aria from a much earlier opera libretto by the Italian poet Pietro Metastasio, sung by a female character who fears she has been abandoned:

Che fa il mio bene?	What is my beloved doing?
Perché non viene?	Why does he not come?
Veder mi vuole languir così?	Does he want to see me to languish like this?
Oh come è lento nel corso il sole!	Oh how slow the course of the sun!
Ogni momento mi sembra un di.	Every moment seems like a day to me.

On the surface, this is a standard lament, the kind of thing found in countless operas. Yet words can convey different meanings according to how we say—or sing—them. Our understanding of such expressions as "Yeah, sure," or "What a surprise!" depends very much on the tone of voice. In this particular case, freed from the contingencies of an operatic plot, Beethoven chose to create two entirely different songs using exactly the same text. The first, marked "Arietta buffa" ("Comic arietta"), is fast and bouncy. Set in the bright major mode and with a busy, scurrying accompaniment throughout, it conveys a tone of exasperation, and the singer's repeated "così" ("like this") at the end, makes the overall effect comic indeed. One has the feeling that the beloved will be in deep trouble when he finally does show up. The second setting, marked "Arietta assai seriosa" ("Very serious arietta"), by contrast, draws on every cliché in the repertory of musical laments: minor mode, slow tempo, grinding dissonances, and a hesitant melodic line with plenty of drooping intervals that mimic a lover's sighs. It is all done to such an extreme, in fact, that we can hear the song either as a lament or as a parody of a lament, overdone to the point of farce. The key word here is "seriosa," which in Italian can mean either "extremely serious" or "overly serious," which is to say, serious to the point of absurdity.

The same word helps explain the unexpectedly sunny ending to the otherwise gloomy String Quartet in F Minor, op. 95, which Beethoven called "Quartetto serioso." After three deeply serious movements Beethoven launches into an equally gloomy finale in a moderate tempo that seems headed inevitably toward a dark conclusion. But just before the end, the music interrupts itself, accelerates to a fast tempo, shifts to the major mode, and introduces an entirely new and jaunty tune that seems diametrically opposed to everything we have heard up to this point. The entire piece is over less than a minute later. This brief ending seems to mock everything that had come before.[9]

In his life as in his music, Beethoven frequently moved without warning between serious and comic, high and low, sublime and slapstick. Even in his performances as a pianist, he could distance himself from his art and draw attention to the craft of manipulating emotions as well as notes. His pupil Carl Czerny recalled how Beethoven could move a roomful of listeners to tears through his improvisations at the keyboard and then afterward mock them for those very tears:

> His improvisation was most brilliant and striking: in whatever company he might chance to be, he knew how to produce such an effect upon every hearer that frequently not an eye remained dry, while many would break out into loud sobs; for there was something wonderful in his expression in addition to the beauty and originality of his ideas and his spirited style of rendering them. After ending an improvisation of this kind he would burst into loud laughter, and banter his hearers on the emotion he had caused in them. "You are fools!" he would say. Sometimes he would feel himself insulted by these indications of sympathy. "Who can live among such spoiled children?" he would cry.[10]

It would be easy to dismiss this as an entertaining yet possibly apocryphal anecdote if it did not resonate with so many moments in music that Beethoven committed to paper, including but by no means limited to the mood-disrupting coda to the finale of the "Serioso" String Quartet. As one French critic so colorfully put it after hearing an unidentified symphony by Beethoven in 1811: "Having penetrated the listener's spirit with a sweet melancholy, he shreds it at once with a mass of barbarous chords. It strikes me as if we were seeing doves and crocodiles penned up together."[11] Or as the pianist Jeremy Denk has noted more recently: "He's a trickster, an unreliable narrator, willing to whip out the rug out from under you, scheming behind your back how to mislead you next."[12] Beethoven could be at once wholly engaged and wholly detached.

Perhaps nowhere is this sense of multiple perspectives more clearly on display than in the String Quartet in B-flat Major, op. 130, a work with two utterly different finales. The original version, from December 1825, ends with a massive fugue that dwarfs all preceding movements in both scale and tone. The Viennese publisher Domenico Artaria recognized the difficulties this extremely long and demanding finale would pose for performers as well as listeners, and for this reason requested (and offered to pay for) a different finale. Beethoven complied, producing a much shorter and lighter movement with driving dance rhythms. Artaria then published the original finale as a separate work of its own, the *Grosse Fuge* ("Great Fugue"), op. 133. It would be cynical to think that Beethoven had created the new finale for money alone: at this late point in his life, he had his choice of commissions. Artaria's offer was unusual in that it gave him an opportunity to end the same work in two different ways. The fact that both finales have their advocates today speaks to the ability of each to close things out convincingly, each in its own way. Nor was the idea of an alternative finale unique to op. 130. According to Czerny, Beethoven at one point even contemplated writing a purely instrumental finale to the Ninth Symphony.[13]

Had he lived longer, Beethoven might very well have carried out this plan. That he would even contemplate the idea speaks volumes about his inclination to adopt contrasting perspectives in any number of situations. This tendency extended at times toward people as well. His correspondence reveals a constant series of turbulent relationships that break and then heal and then sometimes break again. He was quick to change his mind about the loyalty of those around him. The case of Stephan von Breuning is typical. One of Beethoven's closest friends from his Bonn days, Breuning shared a flat with the composer in Vienna for a time in 1804, and in a letter to their mutual Bonn friend Franz Gerhard Wegeler, he described the strain of daily contact, aggravated by the composer's growing deafness. Something must have happened a few weeks later, for in early November Beethoven sent a miniature portrait of himself to Breuning with the wish that what happened between us be concealed forever behind this painting. I know I have wounded your heart. My own emotion, which you certainly must have observed, had punished me enough for it. It was not *malice* within me that was directed toward you; had that been the case I would never be worthy of your friendship. It was passion *in you and in me*—but distrust of you began to stir within me. Individuals came between us, ones who will never be worthy of *you* or *me*. . . . Forgive me if I hurt you; I myself suffered no less when I did not see you for so long beside me. Only then did I realize so vividly how dear you are to *my* heart and always will be.[14]

We can see a similar pattern in other correspondence with Wegeler himself, Eleonore von Breuning, Johann Nepomuk Mälzel, Countess Marie Erdödy, and even Prince Lichnowsky, his most important patron during his early years in Vienna. Beethoven's personal relationships were as mutable as his musical ideas.

He could compartmentalize his creative energies to an astonishing degree. He often worked on several compositions at more or less the same time, rather like those chess masters who take on multiple opponents simultaneously and play each board in sequence. This approach also testifies to his ability to "tune" and "retune" himself in the sense proposed by Friedrich Schlegel: he could enter and leave contrasting musical worlds with apparent ease, no matter how extreme the differences among the various works before him. He reported to Wegeler in 1801 that he often had three or four different compositions in progress at any given moment, and he told a visitor in 1816 that "I don't write anything in one fell swoop without interruption. I always work on many things at the same time. I pick up now this and now that." The sketches for the wholly different Fifth and Sixth Symphonies, composed over the same span of time, certainly confirm this.[15]

Finally, we have Beethoven's own word on the need for composers to be able to step outside themselves when creating new works. He was in a foul mood when he wrote to the publisher Breitkopf and Härtel in February 1812, for Archduke Rudolph, his most important patron in the last two decades of his life, had recently declined his right as coadjutor to become Archbishop of Olmütz, thereby dashing Beethoven's expectations of a stable and highly desirable post at what would have been his patron's new court. He was in such despair at this news that he had to acknowledge his momentary inability to do something that artists in particular must be able to do easily: convey a mood different from that which they actually feel.

> For now I can write only what is absolutely necessary. You say that good humor sparkles in my last letter; artists have to be able to throw themselves often into anything and everything, and so this [good humor], too, might have been feigned, for I am precisely not in good humor at the moment.[16]

This is not to say that Beethoven did not genuinely feel the emotions we hear in his music. That these emotions were routinely imagined makes them no less real for purposes of composing. But composing, for him, was above all a matter of arousing an emotional response in listeners, not of expressing his inner self. He belonged to the last generation of composers who treated instrumental music as a rhetorical art. Rhetoric is the art of persuasion, and composers had long considered it their responsibility (aided by performers) to "persuade" listeners emotionally, to transport them into particular emotional states. The idea that listeners might somehow bear the burden of understanding, that it might be up to them to grasp what a composer was trying to "say," speaks of a mode of listening that would not gain a foothold until later in the nineteenth century. Beethoven's music did in fact become increasingly enigmatic over the course of his life, especially in his last decade, but one of the reasons so many of his contemporaries puzzled over what he had written was that they were simply not accustomed to the notion of listening as an activity that required any special effort on their part.

We routinely accept that responsibility today, and there is nothing wrong with looking to the person of the composer to make sense of what that individual has created. But if our image of that individual lacks depth, our experience of the music suffers. In the case of Beethoven, The Scowl is real enough, but it makes him one-dimensional. It is a caricature, and like any caricature, it exaggerates distinctive features of the individual it portrays. Beethoven scowled but he also laughed, and to judge from contemporary reports, he did so often and quite heartily. Scowling or laughing, he was able to distance himself from his own transitory emotions and create fictional worlds that we as listeners can inhabit at our pleasure.

Chapter 2

The Life

We know more about Beethoven than any composer who lived before him, and for that matter a great many who have come since. The sheer quantity of the historical record can seem overwhelming at times. The correspondence—more than 2,000 letters to and from him—extends across six hefty printed volumes. The document now known as the Heiligenstadt Testament, written in 1802 but secreted away and not discovered until after his death, is a deeply personal and emotionally direct confrontation with the growing reality that he was losing his sense of hearing. In his later years, when his deafness had become severe, visitors often communicated by a combination of shouting and writing, and the 139 conversation books that have survived give us detailed insights into his daily concerns, with entries that range from the mundane to the metaphysical. The diary he kept sporadically between 1812 and 1818 records both philosophical and practical observations. Reminiscences of those who knew him personally fill two substantial volumes. And we have some 8,000 pages of musical sketches that range from brief melodic fragments to extensively drafted complete movements. These sketches allow us to trace the step-by-step growth of many of Beethoven's landmark compositions, along with countless others he abandoned.[1]

We also have to sort through reams of spurious evidence. The first biography, published in Prague shortly after his death and written by one Johann Aloys Schlosser, an otherwise almost completely unknown figure, is full of inaccuracies. In the 1830s, the author Bettina Brentano von Arnim, who knew the composer, published a series of colorful but largely fabricated letters from him and about him. The words she put into Beethoven's mouth are often still repeated as if they were genuine. Anton Schindler, his personal assistant at various times toward the end of his life, published an "I-Knew-Beethoven" biography in 1840 that contains many dubious claims, claims that grew more detailed in a later edition. Scholars have since discovered that Schindler forged entries in the conversation books to make his relationship with the composer seem both longer and closer than it actually was. The fiction surrounding Beethoven's life has consistently reinforced the image of The Scowl, and it has taken on a life of its own. We cannot simply ignore it, for it has shaped the way generations of listeners have heard his music.

The outlines of his life are nevertheless clear enough. Bonn, where he was born on December 16 or 17, 1770, was not a large city, but there was nothing small about it. With a population of just under 10,000, it was the residence of the Archbishop-Elector of Cologne. This was a position that was at once both clerical and political. From 1784 until 1794—Beethoven's formative years—Bonn's ruler was Maximilian Franz, the youngest brother of the Habsburg Emperor, Joseph II. Both brothers were sympathetic to many of the Enlightenment's ideals and encouraged what at the time was a relatively free flow of ideas. Maximilian Franz opened a portion of the palace's library to the public and played a key role in elevating the city's center of learning to the status of a university.

Bonn was also a musically active city, even before the arrival of the music-loving Maximilian Franz from Vienna. Beethoven's grandfather, also named Ludwig, was the court's music director and a prosperous businessman on the side. He had grown up in Mechelen (Malines), in what is now northern Belgium, hence the "van" in the family name. But his only son, Johann, the composer's father, squandered his inheritance, suffered from alcoholism, and neglected his duties as a singer at the court. In 1767 Johann van Beethoven married Maria Magdalena Keverich, a widow, and the couple had seven children, three of whom survived infancy. Their two younger sons, Kaspar Karl and Nikolaus Johann, would eventually follow their older brother to Vienna but were not themselves musicians.

How much older? To the very end of his life, Beethoven seems to have been confused not simply about the day on which he was born—baptized on December 17, he may have been born a day or even two before—but the year as well. Some writers have blamed the confusion on his father, who may have tried to promote him as a child prodigy by shaving a year off the boy's advertised age. Later in his life, Beethoven came to believe that he had actually been born in 1772, even in the face of documented and notarized evidence presented to him on more than one occasion.[2]

In any event, Johann van Beethoven recognized his oldest son's musical abilities early on and saw to it that he received instruction from a series of able teachers. The most notable of these was Christian Gottlob Neefe, who in a report on the musical scene in Bonn in 1783 described his young pupil as a "promising talent" who had already published a set of keyboard variations. "This young genius," Neefe announced, "deserves support that would enable him to travel. He would certainly become a second Wolfgang Amadeus Mozart if he were to make progress in the same way he has already begun."[3]

Beethoven was duly appointed deputy court organist in Bonn in June 1784, his first salaried position. He also played viola in the court orchestra and opera house and in the process acquired first-hand knowledge of the contemporary repertory, most notably symphonies by Haydn and Mozart and operas by Haydn, Mozart, Gluck, and Grétry. He was surrounded by an array of talented young musicians as well, figures who would go on to enjoy eminent careers of their own. These included the composer and theorist Anton Reicha as well as the violinist Andreas Romberg and his cousin, the cellist Bernhard Romberg, both of whom were also composers. Nikolaus Simrock, a somewhat older horn player, would later establish what would become one of the continent's leading music publishing houses.

Though his formal schooling ended sometime around the age of ten, Beethoven remained determined to educate himself throughout his life. He attended lectures at the university, read widely in fields beyond music, and years later would claim that "without making the slightest claim to actual book-learning, there is no treatise that could be too learned *for me*, for from my youth onward I have taken pains to grasp the import of the better and wiser individuals of each age. Shame on any artist who does not consider it an obligation to do at least this much."[4]

But aspirations and accomplishments are two different things, and Beethoven remained painfully aware of his shortcomings in speaking and writing throughout his life. He seems to have learned the use of uppercase letters only in adulthood, and he consistently struggled with numbers. The concept of multiplication eluded him altogether. In one of the conversation books, for example, we can see him adding the number 16 seven times instead of simply multiplying 16×7.[5]

The musical talent, on the other hand, was obvious to all early on. The Elector financed Beethoven's continued musical education in Vienna with the understanding that he would eventually return to service in Bonn. Maximilian Franz was himself a Mozart enthusiast and no doubt saw in the youth the possibility of a second such genius. Indeed, Mozart himself commented in 1782 that the Elector-to-be—still in Vienna at the time—"thrusts me forward on every occasion. And I can say almost with certainty, that if he were already Elector in Cologne, I would also already be his music director."[6] We can only wonder how the history of music would have unfolded if a few years later Mozart had indeed left Vienna for the Rhineland, where he would have met a fourteen-year-old Beethoven.

When Maximilian Franz did finally arrive in Bonn in 1784, he found a well-entrenched music director already in place. With an eye to his new court's musical future, and at the urging of Count Ferdinand Waldstein, one of his advisors, the Elector funded Beethoven's journey to Vienna. In a notebook Beethoven kept at the time, Waldstein wrote this remarkably prescient inscription in late October 1792:

> Dear Beethoven: You are going to Vienna to fulfill your long-frustrated wishes. The spirit of Mozart's genius still mourns and weeps over the death of her pupil. It found refuge but no engagement with the inexhaustible Haydn; through him it wishes once again to be united with someone. With steady diligence, you shall receive Mozart's spirit from Haydn's hands. Your true friend, Waldstein[7]

The "long-frustrated wishes" were a sad fact: Beethoven had already traveled to Vienna once before, in early 1787, with the intention to study with Mozart. While it seems likely they met, there is no documentation to confirm this. That first visit to Vienna had in any case been cut short when Beethoven returned to Bonn to be by the side of his gravely ill mother, who died a few months later.[8] Mozart himself died in December 1791, and so Beethoven turned instead to Haydn, who had himself only recently returned to Vienna from an extended and enormously successful sojourn in London.

Why Vienna? It was widely known as one the most musically vibrant cities in all of Europe, and Maximilian Franz's sponsorship of the young composer assured him of ready access to the city's aristocratic families, who vied with one another to bestow their own patronage on promising young artists. With the exception of opera and sacred music, Vienna's musical life in the 1790s took place largely behind closed doors. There were relatively few truly public concerts, and some of the more affluent aristocrats even maintained their own private orchestras. It was in these salons that Beethoven made his reputation as a composer, virtuoso performer, and above all as an improviser on the piano. In a celebrated "duel" that took place in 1799, he and the pianist Joseph Wölffl took turns improving on themes each provided the other. Years later, the composer Ignaz von Seyfried would recall that "in his improvisations even then Beethoven did not deny his tendency toward the mysterious and gloomy," whereas Wölffl, "trained in the school of Mozart, was always equable; never superficial but always clear and thus more accessible to the multitude."[9]

The dedicatees of Beethoven's early works reflect his ability to attract and cultivate powerful patrons. A composer could not presume to dedicate a publication without the permission of the dedicatee; the dedicatee, in turn, was expected to reward the composer with payment of some kind. A list of the patrons to whom Beethoven dedicated his published works during his first decade in Vienna reads like a Who's Who of the city's aristocracy: princes and princesses, counts and countesses, barons and baronesses, and even the empress herself, Marie Therese.[10]

Prince Karl Lichnowsky was especially generous. A serious music-lover, he established a fund of 600 gulden annually on which Beethoven could draw until such time as he could secure a permanent salaried position. This was no small sum. One contemporary on the scene estimated in 1793 that an unmarried man could live modestly in Vienna on 775 gulden a year, and Beethoven had several other sources of income at the time as well as through teaching, performing, and publishing.[11] Beethoven also received lodging and food in the prince's household, even dining at the prince's table on a regular basis for a time. As a token of thanks, he dedicated a number of major works to Lichnowsky, most significantly the very first of his publications he deemed worthy of an opus ("work") number, the Piano Trios, op. 1, and beyond that the Piano Sonata in C minor,

op. 13 ("Pathétique"), the Piano Sonata in A-flat Major, op. 26, and
the Second Symphony, op. 36.

This seemingly ideal arrangement with Lichnowsky created
problems of its own, however. "Am I supposed to come home daily
at 3:30, change into better clothes, shave, etc.? I can't stand it!" he
declared to one of his friends.[12] And indeed, the more firmly he established himself in Viennese society, the more frequently he refused
entreaties to perform or improvise in the presence of others. This
was the immediate cause of a major break with the prince in 1806,
though the two eventually reconciled. Beethoven struggled all his
life between the financial support he needed and the independence
he craved.

He was not a physically imposing figure. Friends and acquaintances
recall him as stocky, muscular, and of roughly average height for his
time, about 5'5" His sense of rhythm seems to have been entirely in-
ternal. Ferdinand Ries, a former student, would later recall that the
composer was "very clumsy and awkward in his movements; his
gestures were totally lacking in grace. . . . It is difficult to understand
how he succeeded in shaving himself. . . . He could never learn to
dance in time."[13] But he was not indifferent to fashion. Like most of
his generation, he disdained wigs and wore his hair fairly short, an
outward symbol of republican sentiments. A year into his time in
Vienna, he wrote to Eleonore von Breuning back in Bonn requesting
her to knit another waistcoat for him on the grounds that the one she
had given him earlier was now "so unfashionable that I can only keep
it in my closet as something most dear to me from you."[14]

Quite aside from his problems with hearing, he complained
frequently about his health. Gastrointestinal ailments plagued him
constantly. The years took their toll, and when the Englishman John
Russell visited him in 1822, he described Beethoven's "unpromising
exterior" in some detail:

> Though not an old man, he is lost to society in consequence of his
> extreme deafness, which has rendered him almost unsocial. The

neglect of his person which he exhibits gives him a somewhat wild appearance. His features are strong and prominent; his eye is full of rude energy; his hair, which neither comb nor scissors seem to have visited for years, overshadows his broad brow in a quantity and confusion to which only the snakes round a Gorgon's head offer a parallel. His general behavior does not ill accord with the unpromising exterior. Except when he is among his chosen friends, kindliness or affability are not his characteristics. The total loss of hearing has deprived him of all the pleasure which society can give, and perhaps soured his temper.[15]

Nor was he known for his tidiness. One visitor to his two-room flat in 1809 described it as "the dirtiest, most disorderly place imaginable," with moisture on the ceiling and an unemptied chamber pot underneath a piano. The chairs were covered with clothes and with dishes that bore "the remains of last night's supper."[16]

He acknowledged his deafness for the first time in a letter to Wegeler in 1801, but only because Wegeler was in Bonn and not in Vienna. Beethoven wanted his condition kept secret. But by the fall of 1802 he had come to realize that this was no longer possible. While seeking a cure at the spa village of Heiligenstadt, he wrote a long letter to his two brothers that gave voice to his despair. Intended to be read only after his death, the Heiligenstadt Testament is the central verbal document of Beethoven's life. He confessed that the pain of his deafness—both physical and social—was so great that he had contemplated suicide. "It was only *art* that held me back," he declared.

Committing his darkest thoughts to writing at this time seems to have had a cathartic effect. Soon afterward he composed the monumental "Eroica" ("Heroic") Symphony, and over the next ten years he would go on to compose an astonishing number of masterpieces, including the Fourth through Eighth Symphonies, the Fourth and Fifth Piano Concertos, the Violin Concerto, the String Quartets Opp. 59, 74, and 95, and his only completed opera, *Fidelio*.

He created all these works, as well as many of his earlier ones, against a backdrop of war. When the French occupied the Rhineland in 1794, Maximilian Franz had fled to his family home in Vienna. But even there he was not safe from the reach of Napoleon, who would go on to occupy the city twice, first in 1805 without resistance, and then again in 1809 after a bombardment that sent Beethoven to a cellar, clutching pillows to his ears to lessen the pain of the cannon thunder. It was around this time that Beethoven received an invitation from Napoleon's youngest brother, Jérôme, ruler of the newly formed Kingdom of Westphalia, to become music director at the court in Kassel. Beethoven leveraged this offer to secure a generous annuity funded by three Austrian patrons: Prince Lobkowitz, Prince Kinsky, and Archduke Rudolph, with the understanding that he would remain in Vienna.

Beethoven experienced another pronounced deterioration of his hearing beginning around 1812, the year in which he became involved with a woman whose identity remains unknown but whom he called his "Immortal Beloved." The affair was brief but intense. We know of it only from a single letter he wrote to her and which she at some point presumably returned to him. Along with the Heiligenstadt Testament, this letter was discovered only after his death.

The end of this affair—which presumably coincided with the return of the letter—appears to have shaken the composer deeply. He began to keep a diary of sorts shortly afterward, resorting to words once again to help him work through his thoughts at a time of personal crisis. This is not a diary in any conventional sense but rather an unsystematic and occasional collection of jottings and observations, some of them personal, others mundane. It seems to have functioned as the verbal counterpart to the musical sketchbooks, a repository of ideas worthy of further consideration.

The years 1813–15 saw a marked decline in both the quantity and quality of the music he composed. This may have been caused by accelerating deafness, his failed love affair, or some combination of the two. Paradoxically, he was enjoying unprecedented popular success at this moment. In the fall of 1814, leaders and diplomats from all over Europe assembled for the Congress of Vienna, and Beethoven's pocketbook and reputation benefited directly from the many concerts put on to entertain the city's well-heeled visitors. They were there to redraw the continent's boundaries in the wake of Napoleon's defeat, and works such as *Wellington's Victory* and *Der glorreiche Augenblick* ("The Glorious Moment"), written in a more "popular" style than most of his other compositions, won wide critical praise at the time, even if subsequent critics have for the most part preferred to keep their distance from them.

A new phase of Beethoven's life began shortly after the death of his brother Kaspar Karl in November 1815, when he assumed joint legal guardianship of his brother's nine-year-old son, Karl, with the boy's mother, Johanna. There were problems with this arrangement from the start. Beethoven considered his nephew's mother both morally and intellectually deficient, and the two guardians engaged in a nasty five-year court battle over physical custody of the boy. Beethoven eventually prevailed. He carried out his paternal duties conscientiously and devoted countless hours to Karl's upbringing. But the youth's attempted suicide in August 1826 ultimately persuaded the composer to cede guardianship to Stephan von Breuning, who helped secure Karl an appointment in the army.

In spite of these increased demands on his time and energy over the last decade of his life, Beethoven somehow managed to resume his earlier level of intense artistic creativity. "Apollo and Muses will not yet deliver me to the Grim Reaper," he wrote to one of his publishers in 1824, "for I still owe them a great deal, and before I depart for the Elysian Fields, I must leave behind what the spirit provides me and commands me to finish. It really seems to me as if I had written hardly any music at all."[17] At this point Beethoven was in fact in the middle of a five-year span in which he would complete such monumental works as the *Missa solemnis*, the Diabelli Variations, the Ninth Symphony, and the five late string quartets.

But the Grim Reaper did finally call in March 1827. The autopsy report suggests any number of possible causes of death, most of them involving his liver, kidneys, spleen, and pancreas. Franz Grillparzer, one of Austria's leading literary figures, wrote the funeral oration, a noted actor of the time declaimed it, and tens of thousands turned out to witness the procession. "Who shall arise to stand beside him?" Grillparzer asked. The question remains just as relevant today.

Chapter 3

Ideals

Ideals have a way of colliding with reality in every life. In Beethoven's case, the distance between the two was more extreme than most, the collision more severe. His ideals—the principles by which he lived—grew out of a mixture of religious, ethical, and philosophical beliefs. His reality was the need to earn a living in a world of sound he was increasingly unable to hear.

For Beethoven, the one ideal that dominated all others was self-cultivation, or as the German term would have it, *Bildung*. The imperative to develop and realize one's fullest potential, obvious as it may seem to us today, was by no means self-evident in Beethoven's time. His generation in fact witnessed a momentous change in the very conception of the self. The ideal of *Bildung* allowed—indeed, compelled—individuals to explore and exploit those aspects of the self that lay beneath consciousness and apart from the social positions into which they had been born. Its novelty lay not in the belief that each person is unique, but rather that this uniqueness could be cultivated. The term "individualism" was itself an invention of the early nineteenth century.[1]

Beethoven embraced this new sense of self. His correspondence, the Heiligenstadt Testament, and his diary all bear witness to a life-long effort to articulate his vision of what he could become and what he could accomplish. In spite of an only rudimentary formal educa-tion, he read widely and was determined "to grasp the import of the better and wiser individuals of each age."[2] Quotations and allusions sprinkled throughout his correspondence reveal a more than passing acquaintance with such authors as Homer, Plutarch, Shakespeare, Calderón, Herder, Goethe, and Schiller. A French officer who vis-ited him on several occasions in the fall of 1809 reported that the two conversed about "philosophy, religion, politics, and especially of Shakespeare, his idol."[3]

But *Bildung* was about more than knowledge or even self-knowledge: it was above all about the purpose of one's life. Beethoven was aware of his extraordinary musical gifts and saw their realization as his calling. This sense of mission lay at the core of his being and recurs throughout his writings. Anything that impeded his reali-zation of this goal was to be resisted at all costs. Fulfillment of this mission, moreover, required sacrifice. Beethoven recognized that he could achieve his fullest potential only at the cost of foregoing the ordinary pleasures of life, including love. The very first entry of the diary he began to keep in late 1812, shortly after the end of his affair with the Immortal Beloved, reads: "You must not be a *human being, not for yourself, but only for others*: for you there is no longer any hap-piness except within yourself, in your art. O God! Give me strength to conquer myself, nothing at all must fetter me to life."[4]

As if to underscore the centrality of artistic creation to his life, the diary's very next entry reflects on the finer points of voice-leading: "The precise coinciding of several musical voices generally hinders the progression from one to the other." Despair returns with the diary's third entry: "O terrible circumstances, which do not sup-press my longing for domesticity, but [prevent] its realization. O

God, God, look down upon the unhappy B., do not let it continue like this any longer."[5]

The back-and-forth of these opening three entries—from the personal to the technical and back to the personal—captures the inseparability of Beethoven's perspectives on life and music. Only this "divine art," as he put it in 1824, gave him the "lever" and the "power to sacrifice to the heavenly muses the best part of my life."[6] He peppered his diary with self-admonitions to forego earthly pleasures for the cause of art:

> There is much to be done on earth, do it soon! I must not continue my present everyday life; art demands this sacrifice too. Rest and find diversion only in order to act all the more forcefully in art.
>
> If possible, bring the ear trumpets to perfection and then travel. This you owe to yourself, to Mankind and to Him, the Almighty. Only thus can you once again develop everything that has to remain locked within you.[7]
>
> Live only in your art, no matter how limited you are by your senses. This is nevertheless the *only existence* for you.
>
> Sacrifice yet again all the trivialities of social life to your art, O God above all![8]

For Beethoven, art was both a manifestation of the divine and a means by which to approach the divine. He encouraged a young musical admirer not only to practice her art but to "penetrate its interior," for "only art and science elevate mankind to the deity."[9] He made much the same point years later when he wished one of his publishers "every good success for your efforts on behalf of art, for it is only art and science, after all, that point to a higher life and give us hope for it."[10]

Beethoven was scarcely alone in regarding art as a form of religion. German-speakers of the time even coined a word for it: *Kunstreligion*, or "art-religion." By this line of thought, art provided a glimpse of a higher realm beyond the travails of earthly life. And instrumental music, because of its inherently abstract nature, lent itself particularly well to providing intimations of a higher form of existence. Free from the burden of representation and the strictures of language, instrumental music had the capacity to convey what words could not. The poet and dramatist Ludwig Tieck, for example, an acquaintance of the composer, declared the modern symphony to be capable of "delivering" us "to a quiet, happy, peaceful land," and E. T. A. Hoffmann perceived in Beethoven's Fifth Symphony a "wondrous spirit-realm of the infinite."[11]

Art-religion did not supplant the teachings of the church but supplemented them. Beethoven was born into the Catholic faith, and while he was not particularly observant of ritual, he took the Last rites on his deathbed and never expressed the slightest doubt in the existence of a higher power. He regarded Christ as a model of stoicism, and the repeated references and appeals to God in his correspondence rarely come across as formulaic. He considered entrusting his nephew Karl to the care of the noted Catholic theologian and bishop Johann Michael Sailer and annotated heavily his own copy of Christoph Christian Sturm's *Reflections on the Works of God in the Realm of Nature*, a treatise that expounded at length on the reconciliation of science and religion.[12]

But faith for Beethoven went well beyond the church. He seized on any number of belief systems that might help him establish spiritual and ethical coordinates. These included not only Catholicism but also Freemasonry, tenets of various Eastern religions, and pantheism. We should not parse these too closely. He took from each what he found most helpful.

Freemasonry placed special value on the ideal of brotherhood. Beethoven never joined a lodge, for by the time he arrived in Vienna, the golden age of Freemasonry in the imperial city had passed. The order had flourished under the rule of Joseph II in the 1780s, and Mozart and Haydn had both been members. But in the wake of the French Revolution, Emperor Franz II disbanded the lodges on the suspicion that they encouraged revolution, and the movement went underground. Beethoven was nevertheless deeply sympathetic to its basic principles: an obligation to improve one's self, endurance in the face of suffering, and above all the conviction that deeds counted for more than the accident of one's social standing at birth. His network of Viennese friends, patrons, and publishers included many who had previously been active Freemasons, and his correspondence is full of catchphrases that may well have carried Masonic overtones for their recipients. In one particularly curious entry in his diary, Beethoven equates the year 1816 with 5816, an assertion that resonates with the Masonic belief that the world had been created in 4000 BCE.[13]

Eastern religions, the distant (and in many respects imagined) basis for much Masonic doctrine, provided another source of ethical ideals, particularly those associated with stoicism, renunciation, and self-overcoming. Beethoven's engagement with Hindu, Vedantic, and Brahman writings was part of a broader European fascination with Eastern texts that were then being translated and made available for the first time in the West. The diary contains a number of transcriptions from sacred texts, as well as commentaries taken from various German-language books on Eastern religions.[14]

Beethoven was also deeply sympathetic to the idea of pantheism. Nature was for him yet another manifestation of God's presence in the physical world and as such a source of mystical insight. In the countryside, he mused, it was "as if every tree spoke to me: Holy! Holy! In the forest: enchantment! Who can express it all?"[15] On another occasion he claimed that "no one can love the countryside as much as I do. For the forests, trees, and rocks produce the resonance mankind desires."[16] That "resonance" found its own expression in the "Pastoral" Symphony.

Beethoven believed in fate, something never far from his mind. He spoke of it repeatedly in his correspondence and in his diary, always with a sense of reverence. It is never "God's will" but rather something more akin to the ancient Greek concept of an impersonal force, sometimes administered by the gods, sometimes not. Fate plays a major role in the epic poems *Iliad* and *Odyssey*, and Beethoven seems to have appropriated the attitudes of their lead characters as his own. He copied out in his diary the cry of the mortally wounded Hector from Book 22 of the *Iliad*: "But now Fate catches me! Let me not sink into the dust unresisting and inglorious, but first accomplish great things, of which future generations too shall hear."[17] The passage is eerily similar to what Beethoven himself had written in the Heiligenstadt Testament of 1802, in which he confessed to having contemplated suicide in the face of growing deafness but declared that he had held back on the grounds that "it seemed to me impossible to leave the world before having produced everything I felt called upon to bring forth."[18]

Deafness was an agent of fate. Beethoven accepted it but not without a struggle. When he confessed his condition to Wegeler in 1801, he vowed to "grab fate by the throat, it shall certainly not break me completely."[19] He spent years seeking a cure and ultimately concluded that his only option short of suicide was resignation. He called it "a wretched means of refuge" but embraced it because it was the only path by which he could pursue his art. That, in the end, would remain the highest form of self-development and as such his highest ideal.

Chapter 4

Deafness

We will probably never know why Beethoven's hearing began to deteriorate in his late-twenties. Determining the cause of deafness, even in living patients today, can be a challenge: forensic pathologists who have reviewed the symptoms the composer described at various times have suggested at least a dozen possible causes, ranging from a bad fall to rheumatism, typhus, lead poisoning, and various hereditary diseases of the ear.[1]

Beethoven seems to have begun noticing auditory problems sometime around 1798. His pain was both physical and emotional. He confided in 1801 to Franz Gerhard Wegeler, his childhood friend from Bonn, that his ears "whoosh and roar constantly, night and day." He told Wegeler that he had consulted a series of doctors and that they had prescribed various cures for his "horrid condition"—cold baths, lukewarm baths, almond oil, pills, tea poured into the ears—none of which had done any good. For almost two years, he reported, he had avoided social gatherings, for he could not, as a musician, tell people that he was deaf. "What would my enemies—whose numbers are not inconsiderable—say about that?"

To give you some idea of this prodigious deafness, I would tell you that in the theater I have to place myself right next to the orchestra and even lean up against the railing in order to understand the actor. If I am a bit farther away I do not hear the high notes of the instruments or voices. It is remarkable that there are people who have never noticed this in conversation; they believe it's because I so often seemed distracted. . . . Heaven alone knows what will come of this. . . . I have already often cursed the creator and my existence. *Plutarch* has guided me to *resignation*. If it is otherwise possible, I want to defy my fate, even though there will be moments in my life when I shall be God's unhappiest creature.[2]

The composer's anxiety over his growing deafness came to a head in the fall of 1802 toward the end of a months-long stay in the spa village of Heiligenstadt (outside Vienna at the time but now within the city limits). The Heiligenstadt Testament is a remarkable document, one that must have consumed as much of his time and attention as any major composition up to that point. Written in what for him is an exceptionally clear hand, it is almost certainly a clean copy of an earlier, now-lost draft that was presumably full of revisions.

Directed to his two brothers, the document opens with the words "O ihr Menschen"—roughly, "To all humanity." This is in effect Beethoven's apology for himself, an explanation for his antisocial behavior. He laments the loss of the one sense so vital to a musician, a sense he felt he possessed to a degree that "few others in my profession have or have had." He acknowledges that his advancing deafness has driven him from society and made him seem "antagonistic, obstinate, or misanthropic," and he resolves to circulate in society only when he must.

If I approach any gathering of people I am overcome with a deep anxiety for fear of the danger that my condition will be noticed. . . . What a humiliation when someone standing next to me heard a flute from afar and *I heard nothing*; or when someone *heard a shepherd singing* and I heard nothing. Such incidents brought me to the edge of despair; only a little more of this and I should have taken my own life. It was only *art* that held me back. Ah, it seemed to me impossible to leave the world before having produced everything that I felt called upon to bring forth. And so I endured this miserable life, truly miserable. . . . *Patience*, it is said . . . is what I must now choose as my guide. . . . Already in my twenty-eighth year I am compelled to become a philosopher. This is not easy for an artist, more difficult than for just anyone. Lord, you look down on my innermost self; you know and recognize that a love of humanity and a proclivity to good deeds lie there within. O ye who at some point read this, consider that you have done me wrong, and may the Unhappy One console himself by finding one of his kind who in spite of all the impediments of nature nevertheless did everything in his capacity to be accepted into the circle of worthy artists and humans.[3]

The document concludes with brief instructions for the dispersal of his estate after his death and an expression of thanks to his physician and to his principal patron at the time, Prince Lichnowsky. A few days later he added this heartbreaking postscript:

Thus I take leave of you—and unhappily so. Yes, I must now abandon the beloved hope that I brought with me here [to Heiligenstadt] of being healed, at least to some degree. . . . I leave here almost as I came. Even the high spirit that often possessed me in the beautiful days of summer has vanished. O destiny: let a day of pure *joy* appear to me but once. For so long has the inner resonance of joy been foreign to me. Oh when, oh when, Lord, can I find that resonance again in the temple of nature and of mankind? Never? No. Oh, that would be too harsh.[4]

Joy, by this reckoning, would come in the form of "inner resonance," perceived sound. Having completed this highly personal message to posterity, Beethoven locked it away in a secret compartment of his writing desk, where it lay undiscovered until after his death.

As it turned out, his condition would stabilize somewhat in the decade that followed. But the Heiligenstadt Testament was no passing moment of despair: it would prove a roadmap for the conduct of his life. He avoided large gatherings whenever possible and developed ways of coping as needed; his reputation for sullenness and self-absorption no doubt helped in this regard. And he made good on the calling to "bring forth" as much as he could in the time allotted him. The decade that followed was even more productive than the one before.

What was left of his hearing took another sharp turn for the worse around 1812, however. He began using an ear trumpet on occasion—an inverted megaphone inserted into the ear, in effect— and by 1818 had to resort to conversation books, though eyewitness accounts make it clear that he did not always need them. He was never totally deaf, and it is possible he understood certain voices, or voices in certain registers, better than others.

Deafness posed a greater obstacle to Beethoven's career as a performer than as a composer. Widely regarded as one of the city's greatest piano virtuosos, he had to give up performing in public around 1815. He was still playing at private gatherings as late as 1822, but witnesses describe him as playing far too loudly at times and so softly at others that even his listeners could hear nothing.[5] He was nevertheless eager to keep up to date with the latest advances in piano technology. Viennese, French, and English pianos differed in their mechanisms, tone, and range, and he was particularly taken with the English Broadwood that the manufacturer sent him as a gift in 1818.[6] Soon afterward, he began experimenting with an apparatus on top of the instrument, a shell-shaped device that amplified its sound by directing it immediately toward the player seated at the keyboard. Recent hypothetical reconstructions of this resonator have produced intriguing results and help give at least some sense of what Beethoven might have heard while at work on his last three piano sonatas, opp. 109, 110, and 111.[7]

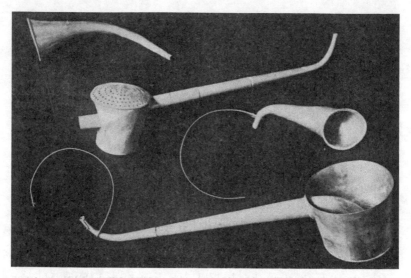

Beethoven used a variety of ear trumpets from 1812 onward and commented at one point about the usefulness of different types for conversation, for the concert hall, and for rooms of different sizes. *Historia/Shutterstock, 7665008na*

Deafness also compromised Beethoven's abilities as a conductor, even if it did not inhibit him from making extreme gesticulations on the podium, as one eyewitness observed in 1814:

> Seized by the power of tones and striving to flow with them, he created a highly interesting spectacle. When the music becomes soft he spontaneously crouches down and keeps things together with a only a faint movement of the arms. When the music gets loud he grapples like a giant with his entire body—he beats, he flails—in short, he is himself the living image of his music.[8]

Entertaining as this display may have been, his technique left much to be desired, and multiple accounts describe the confusion he was apt to sow among an orchestra's players. One performance of *Fidelio* in 1822 was nothing short of a calamity: he was compelled to leave in the middle of the opera and cede the baton to someone else.[9] By the time of the premiere of the Ninth Symphony, he indicated the tempo at the beginning of each movement but did not actually conduct.[10]

How did deafness affect Beethoven's ability to compose? And did it manifest itself in his music? Without downplaying the hardship of his condition, we must keep in mind that composers who have lost their hearing typically retain the capacity to imagine music in their mind's ear: they can still read a score and recreate the sound in their heads. A deaf composer, in other words, is not nearly as remarkable as a blind painter.

As for the effects of deafness on specific compositions, we can only speculate. More than one critic has called attention to the close temporal proximity of the Heiligenstadt Testament and *Christ on the Mount of Olives* (1802). Beethoven's only oratorio, this telling of the Passion story gives unusual prominence to Christ's acceptance of his fate, and the composer must surely have been aware of the parallel to his own suffering.

Deafness would have also aggravated his self-confessed tendency toward melancholy, a condition he complained of as early as 1787 and explicitly portrayed in the finale of his String Quartet in B-flat Major, op. 18, no. 6 (1800), which he labeled "La Malinconia."[11] The labyrinthine progression of increasingly dissonant harmonies at the beginning of this movement, as one scholar has recently suggested, supports the idea that this passage might represent the experience of encroaching deafness. From his many consultations with physicians, Beethoven would undoubtedly have had a basic knowledge of the structure of the inner ear and its labyrinth.[12] The crisis in the finale of op. 18, no. 6, is resolved when the music shifts to a new theme at a fast tempo in the major mode. But the crisis is not resolved in a single step: the slow-moving dissonances return later on, quite unexpectedly, only to be vanquished once again.

This same pattern appears in the finale of the Fifth Symphony (1807), another work that critics have connected to the composer's deafness. One particularly intriguing reading of the work observes that the order in which the wind instruments drop out one by one toward the end of the third movement mirrors Beethoven's own description of his gradual loss of hearing: the flutes, the highest instrument, are altogether absent when the opening theme returns ("what a humiliation when someone standing next to me heard a flute from afar and *I heard nothing*"). The clarinets and oboes, in the middle register, are the next to drop out, leaving at the end only the bassoons, the lowest of the wind instruments. But even these disappear, and toward the end of the movement we hear only the rumbling of the low strings with an odd "croaking" figure that might conceivably approximate the constant rumbling sound he heard in his own ears.[13] This passage of extreme and extended low volume—more than a minute and a half in performance—flows without a break into the finale, whose opening, marked *fortissimo* (extremely loud), introduces instruments not heard before in this work: three trombones, a piccolo, and a contrabassoon. The sudden contrast in volume is overwhelming. The trombones are easily the loudest instruments in the orchestra, and the new winds extend the upper and lower boundaries of the ensemble's register: the piccolo is higher than any instrument we have heard to this point, the contrabassoon as low as the lowest. As in the finale of op. 18, no. 6, the crisis repeats itself: the passage with the ominously low volume from the end of the third movement returns and is followed once again by an overwhelmingly loud fanfare.

More than a few critics have found the tone of this jubilant finale to ring hollow: it is a little *too* jubilant, insisting on a sense of triumph so forcefully and at such length as to call into question the conviction behind its expression. This is a fair criticism, to be sure; again, there are no right or wrong ways to hear this music. But no one would deny the audible trajectory from crisis to triumph, and if we think of the Fifth as an essay in ideals, we can hear it as Beethoven's imagined recovery of his longed-for "inner resonance."

Indeed, the pointed contrasts in volume throughout the Fifth Symphony lend support to Anton Schindler's report of the composer likening the opening motif of the first movement to "fate pounding at the portal." (The common English translation, "Thus fate knocks at the door," misses the violence and scale of the original German: *So pocht das Schicksal an die Pforte.*) This might well be yet another of Schindler's many fabrications. On the other hand, we can speak of emotions in music only metaphorically, and if the "theme" of the Sixth Symphony ("Pastoral") is nature, it is not so far-fetched to think of the Fifth—written at the same time—as an essay on fate and the struggle against it.

Is this how Beethoven intended us to hear these works? Perhaps. But even if one accepts such speculative readings, they do not exhaust the implications of the music. Those who are inclined to search for autobiographical clues in his music are likely to accept Schindler's report about the Fifth Symphony's "meaning." They are also likely to connect that report with Beethoven's promise to "grab fate by the throat" in his 1801 letter to Wegeler in which he confessed his growing deafness.[14] That the context of this vow is medical rather than musical makes no difference to those predisposed to hear the life in the works. The composer's oft-quoted line about fate appears after a long list of health complaints, comments on his current doctor, and queries about Wegeler's opinion of other physicians and possible treatments, including Galvanism, the use of electrical currents to stimulate the auditory nerves. There is not the slightest suggestion that the act of "grabbing fate by the throat" might manifest itself musically. To what extent the composer's personal emotions found their way into his music remains a question that defies any clear answer. As far as his deafness is concerned, we can say with certainty only that his disability helped him—indeed, forced him—to approach his art from a highly uncommon perspective.

Chapter 5

Love

"Beethoven," his student Ferdinand Ries recalled, "was frequently in love, but usually only for a very short time." He appreciated the female form, "especially beautiful, youthful faces."[1] But he never married, and therein lies the tale.

A longing for marriage is a theme that runs throughout his correspondence, at least in earlier years. He proposed or at least seriously considered proposing, in 1810, to Therese Malfatti, the eighteen-year-old daughter of a Viennese banker. Beethoven was close to the family for a time, but for reasons that remain unclear, he was abruptly forbidden access to the household other than for musical occasions. Perhaps Therese's father—or Therese herself—wanted to make it clear that a personal relationship between the two of them had no future.

The composer's most intense love interest, however, was an unidentified woman whose existence is known only through a lengthy three-part letter Beethoven sent her in July 1812. Toward the end of it he calls her "my immortal beloved," and the name, with added uppercase letters, has stuck. The identity of the Immortal Beloved has occupied critics, scholars, and amateur sleuths ever since. Each writer invariably declares the mystery solved beyond all doubt. Just as invariably, another writer reaches a different conclusion with equal conviction.

Among the many candidates proposed over the years are Countess Julie (Giulietta) Guicciardi, Countess Therese Brunsvick, Countess Josephine Brunsvick (her sister), Countess Anna Maria Erdödy, Baroness Dorothea Ertmann, Countess Almerie Esterházy, and Antonie Brentano, née von Birkenstock. (Quite aside from issues of chronology, the idea of the composer's sister-in-law Johanna van Beethoven as the title character of the 1994 film *Immortal Beloved* cannot be taken seriously.) That so many names have been put forward—even this list is selective—gives credence to Ries's recollection that the composer "was frequently in love, but usually only for a very short time"—and, it might be added, with women for whom there was little chance of marriage or a long-term relationship because they were of noble birth, already married, or both. Armchair psychiatrists have had a field day with this, and they have a point, for in a roundabout way, Beethoven's attraction to women who were socially unattainable ensured that a personal attachment to another individual would not in the end conflict with his overriding commitment to his art.

Based on the documentation that has come to light over the years, the two most plausible candidates are Antonie Brentano and Josephine von Brunsvik-Deym-Stackelberg.[2] Whatever the merits of each, the history of the letter and the search for the identity of the Immortal Beloved have much to tell us about Beethoven's side of the affair and about listeners' responses to some of his most famous works.

How did Beethoven come to have this letter—addressed to someone else—in his own possession? It was discovered in a secret compartment of his writing desk after his death, along with the Heiligenstadt Testament. He wanted to keep it, and he wanted it kept a secret, at least as long as he was alive. Either he never sent the letter, or the woman to whom it was addressed returned it to him because she could not risk having it found in her possession. The latter seems the more likely explanation.

The very year in which the letter was written was long a matter of dispute, though scholars now mostly agree that it was written over July 6 and 7, 1812, when the composer was in Bad Teplitz, a Bohemian spa town (now Teplice, in the Czech Republic). The woman's identity revolves around such circumstantial bits of evidence as coach schedules, mail deliveries, and police records that document the arrival and departure dates of visitors to Bad Teplitz and nearby Karlsbad (Karlovy Vary) around that time. The best evidence suggests that Beethoven and the Immortal Beloved had shared a passionate encounter in Prague in early July. Beethoven proceeded from there to Bad Teplitz on July 4, and she departed around the same time for Karlsbad.

Having arrived in Teplitz late the night before, Beethoven began his letter with the words: "My angel, my all, my own self. —Only a few words today, and in pencil (namely yours). . . . Love demands everything, and rightly so, and thus it is *for me with you and for you with me.*" He then related the details of his harrowing two-day, mud-filled journey from Prague. He resumed his letter later that evening, having learned that the mail coach to Karlsbad left only on Monday and Thursday mornings, which meant that it would be several days yet before his Beloved will hear from him. "You are suffering, my dearest creature. . . . Ah, wherever I am, you are also with me, and we speak with each other. I shall arrange it that I can live with you. What a life!!!! thus!!! . . . As much as you love me I love you still more. . . ." And the next morning, he wrote in conclusion:

> Already while still in bed my thoughts rush to you, my Immortal
> Beloved, at times joyfully but then sorrowfully, waiting to learn if
> Fate has heard us. I can live either wholly with you or not at all.
> Yes, I have resolved to wander in faraway places until I can fly into
> your arms and call myself entirely at home with you and can send
> my soul, enwrapped by you, into the realm of spirits. . . . No other

woman than you can possess my heart, none—none. O God, why must one be so separated from what one loves so much? And yet my life in Vienna is a miserable life. Your love makes me at once the happiest and unhappiest of men. . . . Be calm. Only through calm contemplation of our existence can we achieve our goal of living together. Be calm—love me—today—yesterday—what tearful longing for you—for you—for you—my life—my all—farewell— oh continue to love me—never underestimate the truest heart of your Beloved.

L.

Ever yours
Ever mine
Ever ours[3]

Whatever the identity of the "Immortal Beloved," Beethoven's relationship with her shook him to the core. Their affair ended at some point in the second half of 1812, almost certainly broken off by the woman in question. And it was toward the end of that year that the composer began keeping his diary, a document whose first entry concludes with these words: "O God! Give me strength to conquer myself, nothing at all must fetter me to life. In this manner with A everything goes to ruin."[4]

"A" may have been Antonie Brentano, but we know the composer's diary only through transcriptions made by others, and "A" could well be a copyist's misreading of "St," which in turn would point to Josephine von Brunsvick-Deym-Stackelberg.[5] In any case, the end of the affair—and the apparent impossibility of its resumption—made it clear to Beethoven once and for all that domestic bliss was not in his future. If the Heiligenstadt Testament reflects the self-realization that resignation was the only way to deal with his growing deafness, then the diary reflects his resignation to the reality of spending the rest of his life alone. The very fact that he should feel compelled to begin keeping a journal of his private thoughts points to a resolution to open a new chapter in his life and to mark the occasion with a new kind of sketchbook, one that would record his ideas about the conduct of his life in ways both large and small, personal and professional. It is well worth remembering that the diary's second entry addresses technical questions of voice-leading in music. Composition was rarely far from his mind.

How did this affair manifest itself in his music? Anton Schindler, who in 1840 was the first to publish the letter to the Immortal Beloved, maintained that Beethoven possessed the "true soul of an artist" and that this soul manifested itself "to varying degrees in every one of his works."[6] To Schindler's mind, Beethoven's one great love was Giulietta Guicciardi, and the "Moonlight" Sonata of 1802 (*Sonata quasi una fantasia*, op. 27, no. 2) was the composer's musical love letter to her. "What genius," Schindler asked, "could have written the Fantasia in C-sharp minor without such a love? And let it be said here, if only in passing: it was his love for Giulietta, the dedicatee of this work, that inspired him to create it."[7] But Schindler had misdated the letter to the Immortal Beloved, and his hypothesis is now largely rejected. This did not, however, prevent his report from setting in motion a tradition of critical commentary that links this sonata with erotic love. The languorous, plangent first movement of the "Moonlight" Sonata, according to this tradition, embodies longing, its violent finale a renunciation of that longing.[8]

A more plausible candidate for a veiled message to the Immortal Beloved is the 1816 song cycle *An die ferne Geliebte*, op. 98 ("To the Distant Beloved"). It was composed in the same year, after all, that the composer had written to Ries: "*Best greetings to your wife. Unfortunately, I have none, I found only one, whom I shall certainly never possess. I am nevertheless no misogynist.*"[9] The Immortal Beloved was still clearly on his mind some four years after the end of the affair, and this is indeed an unusual work, the most innovative of all his compositions for voice and piano. It is not merely a collection of songs but the first true song cycle, in which the individual numbers move through a quasi-narrative sequence and even share musical motifs in subtle ways. What makes the set even more unusual is that Beethoven directs the six songs to be performed continuously, without a pause between them. (He would later use this same strategy in the seven-movement String Quartet in C-sharp minor, op. 131.)

New research has shown that the song cycle's beloved is distant because she is deceased. It now seems clear that the cycle was commissioned by Prince Lobkowitz as a memorial to his late wife, Maria Karoline. In the opening song, the "hill" on which the singer tells us he is sitting is a metaphor for a grave, and the title page indeed shows a male lutenist singing to a distant female figure high up in the clouds.[10] The motivation behind the commission does not in any way preclude the idea that Beethoven thought of his own Immortal Beloved in composing this work. Compositional treatises had long

The title page of *An die ferne Geliebte* ("To the Distant Beloved"), op. 98 (Vienna: S. A. Steiner, 1816). Long thought to be associated with the "Immortal Beloved," this song cycle was in fact a memorial to the late wife of the dedicatee, Prince Lobkowitz. *Courtesy of the University of North Carolina at Chapel Hill Music Library*

emphasized that in order to project an emotion, a composer must have had some personal experience of it, and Beethoven's music is undoubtedly the richer for the intensity of the affair. Yet we should remain wary of assertions that insist on drawing direct lines between any of his various relationships and specific works of music. In this sense, the affair with the Immortal Beloved was an important event that shaped his larger vision of life, which in turn contributed to the more specific vision of his art.

Chapter 6

Money

Money was a source of constant anxiety for Beethoven, and understandably so, for when it came to making a living as an independent composer, his ideals collided with reality in ways that were at times brutal. Throughout his career he sought a fixed court position that would assure him a steady and reliable source of income. He failed at every turn.

Bad timing played a major role. Beethoven came of age in an era when court appointments of the kind he desired were rapidly becoming extinct. Two decades of war and inflation had drained the coffers of those aristocratic families that had grown accustomed to employing their own private orchestras and the directors to lead them. Haydn, almost forty years older than Beethoven, had made his career in a very different musical world. He had spent nearly three decades as *Kapellmeister*—"master" of the *Kapelle*, the ensemble of instrumentalists and singers—for a single noble family, the Esterházys. In their winter palace in Vienna and summer palace in what is now Hungary, Haydn had at his disposal what was by all accounts one of the leading orchestras of Europe, supported by a prince both willing and able to spend lavishly on his court's musical

life. The summer palace even had its own opera house and mario-
nette theater.

Haydn was responsible for all aspects of music at the court: hiring
and firing, rehearsing, performing, composing. "My prince," as he
told one of his biographers late in life, "was satisfied with all my
works, I received applause, and as the director of an orchestra I could
make experiments and observe what elicited or weakened an impression and thereby improve, add, delete, take chances. I was cut off
from the world; no one in my vicinity could cause me to doubt myself and torment me, and so I had to become original."[1] There were
drawbacks to this arrangement, to be sure: it was not until the 1770s
that Haydn received permission to sell his own compositions, and
even as late as 1790 he was still chafing at the prince's restrictions
on his freedom to travel. But he enjoyed a steady income and could
concentrate on his work. These were precisely the goals that would
elude Beethoven.

They had eluded Mozart for the most part as well. After moving
to Vienna in 1781 he repeatedly sought a permanent appointment
of some kind but could do no better than a minor and essentially
part-time position at the imperial court. The responsibilities were
few, the pay was modest, and the inevitable palace intrigues did
not help. In the end, Mozart had to string together an income from
his published music, performances of his operas, concertizing, and
giving private lessons.

For all his connections at court and among the aristocracy,
Beethoven was even less successful. He assured the publisher
Franz Anton Hoffmeister in 1803 that he would gladly convey to
him all his new works to publish if that alone would assure him of
sufficient income. "Yet consider that everyone around me holds
appointments and knows exactly what they have to live on. But
Good Lord! Where would one appoint such a *parvum talentum
quam ego*—at the Imperial Court?"[2] There is a distinct tone of bit-
terness beneath Beethoven's self-deprecatory jest about his "small
talent." Quite aside from a lack of long-term financial security, he

resented the incalculable hours devoted to what he called the "sour business" of haggling over fees with publishers. In another letter to Hoffmeister he sketched out a possible way to avoid this: a "store-house of art" (*Magazin der Kunst*) to which "the artist would only have to hand over his works in order to take in return what he needed."[3] Commentators have since noted the congruence of this scheme with Karl Marx's later dictum "from each according to his ability, to each according to his needs." Beethoven knew full well that this was another one of his utopian ideals and altogether unwork-able, especially in Vienna in the early 1800s.

In the meantime, he mused in his diary about traveling and eventually securing a position at "a small court" with a "small mu-sical ensemble," and performing there "the hymn to the glory of the Almighty, of the eternally infinite." On another occasion he entertained the idea of serving at the court of Napoleon in Paris.[4] Even as late as 1822, when he learned about the death of Anton Teyber, the Habsburg court composer, he was making inquiries behind the scenes about securing an appointment as Teyber's successor.

The only meaningful offer Beethoven ever received came in October 1808, not from Napoleon but from Napoleon's youngest brother, Jérôme, ruler of the newly formed Kingdom of Westphalia. For all his claimed indifference to titles and nobility, Beethoven became quite agitated when the press reported the nature and circumstances of the offer incorrectly. He wrote to the editors of Leipzig's *Allgemeine musikalische Zeitung* asking them to set the re-cord straight:

> I thank you for the article ... but I request that you at some point correct the matter as concerns [the composer Johann Friedrich] *Reichardt*. I was not in any way engaged by him. To the contrary, it was the Chief Chamberlain of His Majesty the King of Westphalia, Count Truchsess-Waldburg, who arranged to have the offer made to me, and specifically as *Chief Kapellmeister* of H[is] M[ajesty] of

Westphalia. . . . At the next opportunity . . . you should present the
truth about the matter, *for it is vital for my honor.* . . . I laugh at such
matters, but there are those *misérables* who know how to cook up
and serve such things.[5]

Beethoven clearly placed great weight on exactly who made the
offer to him and the exact title of the position: he writes "erster
Kapellmeister"—"first" or "chief" music director—in large letters
and underlines each word three times. His claim that he "laughs"
at such things rings hollow, given his table-pounding insistence that
the record be corrected.

In the end, Beethoven declined Jérôme's offer and leveraged it
for the annuity of 1809 that kept him in Vienna. For the moment,
at least, he seemed to have achieved his goal of a steady income, and
better still, without the responsibilities that came with any court position. The reality of the arrangement played out quite differently.
Only Archduke Rudolph paid his share from the start; contributions
from Princes Kinsky and Lobkowitz got tied up in legal battles that
dragged on for six years before being settled; and inflation ate away
at the original value of the fund. Over the long term, the annuity did
provide a steady source of income but one smaller than Beethoven
had at first anticipated and in any case insufficient by itself to support him adequately, even according to his own relatively modest
standard of living. In the end, he was able to afford a servant and
cook, and though he had to borrow funds from time to time, he was
always able to repay his debts. He even lent money on occasion,
most notably to his brother Kaspar Karl.

Like Mozart before him, Beethoven had to make his living by
drawing on a variety of sources. Beyond the support of patrons—
the grant from Prince Lichnowsky early on, the annuity of 1809
later—his primary sources of income were performing, teaching,
commissions, and sales of his published works. Performing—
both in public and in private—could be lucrative if unpredictable
and sporadic. Particularly in his early years in Vienna, Beethoven

played the piano frequently in the palaces of his aristocratic patrons and received some form of payment in return. He also organized a number of occasional concerts ("academies," as they were called) for a ticket-buying public that would have included many of those same aristocratic patrons. Beethoven typically served as impresario, composer, conductor, and piano soloist at these events and kept the profits for himself after covering the expenses. For his first such production, in 1800—"the most interesting academy in quite a while," one contemporary reviewer remarked—he rented out one of the city's major theaters, hired an orchestra, and presented a program that paid homage to his two great predecessors in the form of a symphony by Mozart and two arias from Haydn's *Creation* but otherwise consisted entirely of his own works: the Piano Concerto no. 1, op. 15; the Septet, op. 20; an improvisation at the keyboard; and as a grand finale, the premiere of the First Symphony.

More ambitious still was the academy of December 22, 1808, in the Theater an der Wien. Its all-Beethoven program consisted of the Fourth Piano Concerto (with the composer as soloist), the concert aria "Ah, perfido!" op. 65, the Gloria and Sanctus from the Mass in C, op. 86, a solo improvisation on the piano, and the premieres of the Fifth and Sixth Symphonies. As if all this were not enough, the evening concluded with the premiere of the Choral Fantasy, op. 80. But there things went off the rails. Beethoven had to stop the performance in order to get all the musicians on the same page. He later apologized for humiliating them, who, like the audience, had had to endure not only Beethoven's temper but also four hours of bitter evening cold. The composer Johann Friedrich Reichardt stayed to the end and concluded that one could have "too much of a good—and beyond that, powerful—thing."[6]

Beethoven did not like teaching: he considered it a drain on his time and energy. Even in his early years in Vienna he took on only a few piano students and in 1801 a single composition student, Ferdinand Ries, the son of a family friend from Bonn. Ries also doubled as the composer's personal assistant for the next several

K.K.P. THEATER AN DER WIEN.   №68.   THÉATRE I.R.P. À LA VIENNE.

Vienna's Theater an der Wien was the site of Beethoven's "academy" of December 22, 1808, which included the public premieres of the Fifth and Sixth Symphonies, the Fourth Piano Concerto, and the Choral Fantasy. In 1803–4 Beethoven lived in a flat that was part of the theater complex. *Wien Museum*

years. Beethoven's only other composition student, from about 1809 onward, was the Archduke Rudolph, a more-than-competent composer and by all accounts an excellent pianist. Theirs was an unusual relationship, for he was a patron as well as a student. Small wonder that Beethoven should dedicate some of his most important works to him, including the Piano Concertos opp. 58 and 73 ("Emperor"), the Piano Sonata op. 81a ("Les Adieux"), the Violin Sonata op. 96, the Piano Trio op. 97 ("Archduke"), the Piano Sonatas opp. 106 ("Hammerklavier") and 111, the *Missa solemnis*, op. 123, and the *Grosse Fuge*, op. 133. The relationship was complicated still further by Rudolph's familial connections to the very center of power at the Habsburg court, for he was the youngest brother of the emperor Franz I. Two themes emerge from the correspondence: gratitude and resentment. On the one hand, Beethoven was grateful for the archduke's steadfast support for the 1809 annuity and for the payments he received for lessons. More important still was the prospect of a permanent court position. Yet he begrudged the time devoted to lessons and especially resented the idea of being available at a moment's notice to accommodate the archduke's schedule.

Finally, Beethoven's own compositions: these produced income in multiple ways. The dedicatee of any new work would typically reward the composer with some sort of payment. Prince Lobkowitz, for example, gave the composer 400 gulden in return for the dedication of the "Eroica" Symphony, along with exclusive rights of performance by the prince's own private orchestra for half a year. That sum alone represented two-thirds of the annual support he was receiving at the time from Prince Lichnowsky. There was also the occasional commission, such as Count Razumofsky's request for three string quartets (op. 59), Prince Nicolaus II Esterházy's call for a setting of the Mass (op. 86), or Prince Galitzin's invitation for "one, two, or three new string quartets," which eventually became opp. 127, 130, and 132. Beethoven could also solicit subscriptions—advance purchases—for new works, as he did in the case of the op. 1 Piano Trios and the *Missa solemnis*.

Beethoven assured publishers on more than one occasion that he did not write for money alone, but in the next breath would almost invariably try to negotiate a higher payment. And he would occasionally sell the same work to more than one publisher. While this might strike us today as unethical, we should remember that there was no effective system of international copyright at the time, and that publishers themselves often issued pirated editions of their own. Great Britain, in particular, functioned as a largely separate market from that on the continent, and Beethoven did a lively business with British publishers.

He also had to think about which genres would work "more or less" to his advantage, as he confessed to the publisher C. F. Peters. In a half-joking, half-serious letter of 1818 to his friend the cellist Vincenz Hauschka, he reported from rural Mödling, outside Vienna, that he was

> . . . rambling about in the mountains, ravines, and valleys here with a piece of music paper, smearing various things on it for the sake of bread and money, for I have reached such heights in this all-powerful former Land of the Phaeacians that in order to gain some time to write a great work I must first do a vast amount of scribbling for the sake of money so that I can survive while writing a great work.[7]

The category of "great" or "large" works (*grosse Werke*) played a key role in Beethoven's vision of his calling. While the dividing line between these and presumably "lesser" genres is not always clear, he seems to have thought of symphonies, masses, and operas as qualitatively different from sonatas, string quartets, or songs. He repeatedly expressed the wish to devote himself to large-scale works even while recognizing the far greater public demand for compositions in smaller genres. "My situation demands that I take every advantage into consideration," he wrote to C. F. Peters, one of his publishers, in 1823. Once he had resolved to work in a particular genre, however, he focused on the task at hand. "Thank God I never think about the advantage" in writing smaller-scale works, he assured Peters, "but only about how I write."[8]

This was true enough. His contemporary detractors complained repeatedly about the difficulty of his music, no matter what the genre, and even his supporters conceded that his works were challenging for performers and listeners alike. From a purely technical point of view, his music was hard to play. And it ran counter to conventions so often that listeners had trouble absorbing it. Beethoven knew this. As he wrote to the pianist and composer Andreas Streicher in 1796,

"I am satisfied even if only a few understand me."[9] This is a long way from his teacher Haydn's alleged (and widely circulated) statement that his own musical language was "understood throughout the world."[10] It also contradicts the spirit of Mozart's oft-quoted assertion that he had written a set of three piano concertos in such a way as to appeal to connoisseurs and amateurs alike.[11] In this respect Beethoven's attitude was radical. He could not and did not ignore the music-consuming public's tastes and abilities altogether, but he did challenge them repeatedly.

This came at the cost of bad notices. Reviewing a set of early variations issued in 1799, one critic sniffed that "Herr Beethoven may be able to fantasize, but how to vary is something he doesn't understand well." The variations, in other words, were so imaginative that they departed unrecognizably (and thus unacceptably) from the original theme. The set as a whole, moreover, was marred by "ugly" dissonances and a generally "labored" nature.[12] Another critic that same year took the composer to task for "going his own peculiar way" in the three Violin Sonatas of op. 12. "And what a bizarre, cumbersome way! . . . A hunt for unusual modulations, a loathing for conventional transitions, a piling up of difficulty upon difficulty to such an extent that one loses all patience and joy in the process."[13] And these, it should be noted, were responses to works that today are scarcely considered to be among the composer's more innovative.

Reviews of this kind from Beethoven's day are too common to be ignored or dismissed simply as the product of small minds. Then, as now, there was the occasional dullard critic, but listeners of the time simply did not consider it their responsibility to make sense of what a composer had written. The composer's obligation, as they saw it, was to satisfy listeners, not puzzle them. In retrospect, then, we can see that Beethoven's career coincided with a period of transition in the history of listening, for the idea of listeners making an effort to grasp the thought of a composer would not become common until later in the nineteenth century.[14]

Negative reviews also inevitably cut into sales. "Advise your reviewers to show more discretion and intelligence," Beethoven wrote to the editors of Leipzig's leading music journal in 1801.[15] And critics did in fact adjust gradually. They initially regarded the "Eroica" Symphony, for example, as diffuse and overly long, but it became an audience favorite within a few years. By the end of the composer's life, only the works of the "late" period continued to puzzle audiences, though by that point at least some critics were willing to give the composer the benefit of the doubt. One reviewer who could make no sense of the *Grosse Fuge*, op. 133, called it "incomprehensible, like Chinese," but hastened to add that "we nevertheless do not want to dismiss things too hastily. Perhaps the time will come when that which on first sight seemed to us opaque and muddled will be recognized as clear and pleasing forms."[16] The allusion to the words of Saint Paul in 1 Corinthians 13:12 ("For now we see through a glass, darkly; but then face to face") suggests that Beethoven's music had by now achieved the kind of respect normally accorded Holy Writ.

Chapter 7

Politics

Beethoven was born into—and died in—a world of strict social hierarchies. The most fundamental division was that between nobility and commoners. Each of these realms in turn had its own defined strata, from emperors to common nobility, from affluent merchants to common laborers. Musicians occupied a roughly middle position in the ranks of the non-nobility. Society regarded them as highly skilled craftsmen. Those who, like Beethoven's grandfather, rose to the position of *Kapellmeister*—musical director—could generally count themselves among the highest-paid members of a court's staff.

Beethoven was also born into a world in social and political flux. He was eighteen years old when the French Revolution broke out, and he witnessed changes that transformed not only the map of Europe but its mind as well. Small wonder, then, that his own political views so often seem contradictory. His attitude toward Napoleon, the most important political figure of the day, lurched from one extreme to the other. He was inspired by the French leader's ideals and planned to dedicate the Third Symphony to him, at one point even calling the work "Bonaparte." But at some point—possibly when he learned in 1804 that the First Consul had crowned himself emperor—he canceled the name so violently on one copyist's manuscript that his quill ripped a hole in the paper and he renamed the work *Sinfonia eroica* ("Heroic Symphony").

But now the contradictions begin. He later added in pencil at the bottom of the same manuscript's title-page "Geschrieben auf Bonaparte" ("Written on Bonaparte"). He suffered tremendous pain in his ears when Napoleon's troops bombarded Vienna in May 1809 and in a marginal note to the score of the Fifth Piano Concerto, which he began sketching around the same time, observed that "Austria owes Napoleon payback."[1] A few weeks later he asked a visiting French officer if he thought Napoleon would receive him in Vienna and soon afterward gave serious consideration to becoming *Kapellmeister* to Napoleon's brother at the court of the Kingdom of Westphalia. The following year he contemplated dedicating his Mass in C, op. 86, to Napoleon. Then in 1813 he wrote the hugely popular *Wellington's Victory*, an orchestral work that portrayed in graphic musical detail one of Napoleon's key defeats. A year later he contributed to the celebrations surrounding the Congress of Vienna, which established a blueprint for post-Napoleonic Europe.

What are we to make of so many contradictions? Once again, Beethoven's ideals had collided with reality. Almost everything he said or did about politics has to be evaluated through the prism of his overarching drive to fulfill his calling to compose. He embraced the core ideals of the French Revolution—liberty, equality, and fraternity—and was appalled when Napoleon's actions violated them. Higher still, though, was his own vision to produce everything he "felt called upon to bring forth," as he had put it in the Heiligenstadt Testament of 1802. This objective took precedence over all else, and by 1809 he had come to realize that an appointment as *Kapellmeister*, no matter how imperfect the court, offered the best path to his goal. The ruler at his own court in Vienna, after all, was scarcely a paragon of liberty, equality, or fraternity.

Tempting as it might be, then, we should not read too much of Beethoven's personal views into the seemingly "reactionary" pieces he wrote for the Congress of Vienna: the cantata *Der glorreiche Augenblick* ("The Glorious Moment") and the chorus *Ihr weisen Gründer glücklicher Staaten* ("Ye Wise Founders of Fortunate Nations"), both to texts lauding the assembled rulers, and *Germania*, for bass solo, chorus, and orchestra, a rousing paean to an imagined German state. True to form, Beethoven viewed the whole affair from multiple perspectives. He recognized the opportunities the Congress would present in the form of commissions, which he duly fulfilled, and of potential gifts, which he duly received. The empress of Russia, impressed by works like the Seventh Symphony and *Wellington's Victory*, sent him a gift of 200 gold ducats—roughly twice the annual income of an experienced musician at the court opera—and he reciprocated by dedicating to her his Polonaise for piano, op. 89.[2]

He also knew that these illustrious visitors would need to be entertained. The prestigious Kärntnertor Theater presented *Fidelio* some thirty times between May 1814 and July 1815, and Beethoven gave no fewer than three academies over the course of the Congress. The last of these was a benefit concert for the almshouse of Saint Marx, conducted by the composer himself. In recognition of this act of generosity, the City of Vienna granted him honorary citizenship.[3]

Beethoven was also able to take a more jaundiced view of things. As he wrote in the fall of 1814 to the lawyer Johann Nepomuk Kaňka in Prague, himself an amateur composer and pianist: "As you yourself know, the creative spirit must not be shackled by the miserable needs of life. . . . I shall report nothing to you of our monarchs, etc., our monarchies, etc. The newspapers will tell you everything. The empire of the mind (*das geistige Reich*) is the one dearest to me and the one superior to all spiritual and secular monarchies."[4]

The "empire" of *Geist*: the German noun is notoriously untranslatable. "Mind" is probably the best we can do in English, but it goes far beyond intellect to encompass the spirit or soul, as well as a certain sense of verve and wit, what the French call *ésprit*. And as far as *Geist* was concerned, Beethoven considered himself superior to any and all members of the nobility, for his was a nobility of the spirit. "As for 'being noble,'" he wrote to Schindler in 1823, "I believe I have sufficiently shown you that I am so in principle."[5] Like so many noblemen, he also had no difficulty looking down on commoners. In August 1794 he reported to his friend Nikolaus Simrock in Bonn that "important persons here have been locked up; there was supposed to have been a revolution. But I believe that the Austrian will not revolt as long as he has his *brown ale* and *sausages*."[6] And in the much later legal battle over guardianship of his nephew, he wanted nothing to do with the city's court for commoners, which he dismissed as suitable only for "innkeepers, cobblers, and tailors." He certainly never corrected those who mistook the "van" in his name—a common surname prefix in the Low Countries—for "von," an indicator of nobility in German-speaking lands.[7]

In practice, Beethoven had to navigate carefully among his noble patrons, even as they negotiated their own dealings with him, for patronage was a mutually beneficial relationship: he used the nobility to enhance his reputation and income, and the nobility used him to enhance its cultural prestige.[8] Music-making was an important feature of life in Viennese salons, and his ready-made connections to the court through the early patronage of Maximilian Franz helped him establish his footing in the upper echelons of Viennese society with relative ease.

Maintaining those connections over the long term proved more difficult. For all the nobility's professions of friendship and affection, distinctions of class inevitably arose and grated on the composer time and again. A romantic attachment to any patron's daughter was out of the question: he was not one of their kind. And he resented in particular the slightest hint of servitude. Even Prince Lichnowsky, who had been so extraordinarily generous to him for so many years, fell victim to the composer's sensitivity on this point. While entertaining a group of French officers at his Silesian estate in 1806, the prince asked Beethoven to perform at the piano. He refused, tensions escalated, and he left the estate that night in a rage. Back in Vienna, he smashed his plaster bust of Lichnowsky by throwing it to the floor, declaring: "The nobility are all dogs!"[9]

Napoleon's conquest of Vienna in May 1809 brought politics closer to home in even more tangible ways. The battles fought just across the Danube, at Aspern-Essling (an Austrian victory), and at Wagram (a decisive Austrian defeat) filled the city with wounded and dying soldiers. Casualties from Wagram alone are estimated to have been around 72,000, the costliest battle in European history up to that point. "What a destructive, desolate life around me," Beethoven reported to a publisher in Leipzig. "Nothing but drums, cannons, and human misery of all kinds. My current situation compels me once again to haggle with you."[10]

Like many of his musical colleagues in Vienna, Beethoven was caught up in the patriotic fervor sweeping the city, and he capitalized on it. He wrote several marches for military band and started to make a setting of the poet Heinrich Joseph von Collin's "Österreich über alles" ("Austria above All Else"). The events of the day found their way into his Piano Sonata in E-flat, op. 81a, through its title, "Les Adieux" ("Farewell"), and its movement headings, which reflect the departure of Archduke Rudolph from Vienna in advance of the approaching French troops on May 4, 1809 (the first movement), his absence over the ensuing months (the slow movement), and his return on January 30, 1810 (the finale). The opening notes of the first movement's slow introduction are even underlaid with the German word "Lebewohl" ("Farewell").

Critics have often pointed to this sonata as Exhibit A in drawing direct connections between Beethoven's life and works. In truth, it reminds us that the motivations behind any given composition could be multilayered. We now know that the title and descriptive movement headings were added after the music had already been written.[11] The entire sonata conforms to the standard format of the genre: a fast first movement is followed by a slow, contemplative

middle movement, and the whole concludes with a fast, jubilant finale. Aside from the opening slow introduction (in itself not unusual), the bulk of the first movement is quite lively and spry.

The sonata thus masks a more complicated relationship with
a member of the royal family and by extension, with royalty in general. In a remarkably blunt note to himself on a sketch leaf from
October 1810—just a little more than eight months after Archduke
Rudolph's return to Vienna—Beethoven memorialized his thoughts
on the matter: "It should be clear enough to you for all time that the
requirement to be near the Archduke always puts you in the most
tense state, hence the gout-like constraint when staying with him in
the countryside. There is always a tense relationship, and this is not
suitable for a true artist, for the artist can be a servant only to the
muse he worships."[12]

Nor does the situation seem to have changed much over the next
decade. In 1818 he wrote to his former pupil Ferdinand Ries, who
was by this time in London, that "my unfortunate connection to
this Archduke has brought me close to *beggardom*; I can't see myself
starving, I have to give in. So you can contemplate how I suffer all
the more in these circumstances!"[13]

Beethoven could not afford to say such things in public to friends
in Vienna, for police and paid informants were part of everyday
life. Censorship had become increasingly stringent under the rule
of the emperor Franz and all the more so later under the eye of his
close advisor, Clemens von Metternich, the chancellor of state.[14] If
the ideals of the French Revolution were to be suppressed, public
discourse of all kinds had to be monitored and regulated. The text
for the opera *Leonore*—which eventually became *Fidelio*—aroused
deep suspicion from authorities on multiple occasions. Joseph
Sonnleithner, who had transformed an earlier French text into the
libretto, conceded in his appeal to the censors that the plot did indeed involve a government official who had abused his power, but
he pointed out that this was "only a matter of personal revenge—
in Spain—in the sixteenth century," and that the villain was

subsequently "punished by the court," with the whole juxtaposed against the "heroism of female virtue."[15] Spain was a conveniently remote setting for stage productions that portrayed the ruling class in a light that was anything less than noble. Like Mozart's *Marriage of Figaro* and *Don Giovanni*, Beethoven's *Fidelio* was set there, and at a temporal remove far from the present. In the end, moreover, it is an enlightened ruler, the minister of state Don Fernando, who saves the day by liberating those unjustly imprisoned.[16]

The conversation books abound with grumblings—by Beethoven as well as his companions—about the climate of repression. At one point his young assistant, Karl Holz, observed that "One has to travel to North America to give one's ideas free rein."[17] In another entry, the composer's nephew Karl admonished the composer not to be so open about his opinions in the coffee houses where Beethoven liked to spend afternoons with friends or a newspaper: "Silence! The walls have ears."[18] But the police on the whole gave Beethoven a fairly wide berth, in part because of his fame, in part because they regarded him as something of an eccentric, in part because they believed that instrumental music posed no threat to the social order.

Or so they thought. In one especially intriguing entry in a conversation book from 1823, the poet and playwright Franz Grillparzer told the composer that "the censor cannot hold anything against musicians. If they only knew what you think about in your music!"[19] Among cognoscenti at least, instrumental music in general and symphonies in particular were in fact regarded as sublimated forms of public expression. They likened the symphony to an ideal society in which each instrument contributed its own distinctive voice to a harmonious whole.[20] Though the political content of any given symphony might be opaque, the very act of performing one constituted a political statement of its own kind. Beethoven would take full advantage of this in his Ninth Symphony, with its message of joy as a unifying element of all humanity.

Chapter 8

Composing

The act of artistic creation of any kind is a process shrouded in mystery, and perhaps nowhere more so than in the realm of purely instrumental music, the kind on which Beethoven's reputation has always rested. A composer setting a text to music—as in a song or an opera—begins with something definite, a text that suggests a certain kind of mood and perhaps even certain rhythms. A composer writing a sonata, string quartet, or symphony, by contrast, begins with nothing. To all outward appearances the music comes from nowhere, which is to say, from within.

We nevertheless have a good sense of how Beethoven went about composing, thanks to the many sketchbooks he left behind. He began by jotting down musical ideas as they came into his head. These were sometimes little more than a few intervals and rhythms, but if they passed muster he would begin to explore their possibilities and develop them. Thinking and writing went hand in hand, and what in the end might seem like the simplest of melodies were often those that required the greatest labor. He tried out some nineteen different versions of what would become the "Ode to Joy" melody of the Ninth Symphony before settling on just the right one.[1] As ideas for a movement or work began to accumulate, he would create what scholars have come to call a continuity draft, a rudimentary roadmap, as it were, of the movement or piece as a whole. When things had gotten far enough, he would transfer this skeletal outline onto proper full-sized music paper and expand the material into a complete score with all its parts. He would then hand the score over to a copyist, who would prepare a clean version, which in turn was subjected to further review and revisions by the composer before going off to a publisher to be engraved.

Beethoven's study, sketched shortly after his death by J. N. Hoechle. Manuscripts cover the piano and the books are in disarray on the shelves. *Wien Museum*

Beethoven used two different kinds of sketchbooks. The desk sketchbooks stayed at home: these are mostly in oblong format, and he wrote in them in ink. The pocket sketchbooks, by contrast, were small enough to take on walks, and he would typically write in these in pencil. Paper was relatively expensive, and although he sometimes bought ready-made gatherings of lined music paper, he often assembled sketchbooks himself by sewing together individual leaves of roughly the same size. He took enormous care to preserve them, more care in fact than he took with his finished scores once they had been published. He presumably referred to these sketches from time to time, though to what extent he actually did so remains unclear.

From the middle of the nineteenth century down to the present, scholars have devoted countless hours to transcribing and interpreting these sketches. This has been a daunting task, given the composer's notoriously difficult scrawl, compounded by the fact that these sketches were never intended for any eyes other than his own. Through these transcriptions, we can now reconstruct in remarkable detail the genesis and growth of a good many works and watch their creation unfold, sometimes smoothly, more often not. The sketchbooks preserve many false starts, with perhaps as many as fifty symphonies begun but soon abandoned.[2] The toils so evident in these volumes have certainly reinforced the perception of Beethoven's art as a reflection of his life. They are, as one scholar has observed, "artifacts of the struggle."[3]

Yet something vital is missing from these sketches, what might be called the aha! moment. We have a record of the before and after but not of the moment of inspiration itself, the shift from something perfectly correct to something remarkable, from something inchoate to something formed. The sketches thus remind us of that fuzzy line that divides inspiration from reflection, imagination from the technical craft of composition.

It is not enough, after all, to come up with a good melody or a catchy motif: these have to be sustained and developed in some way, for the ear tolerates only so much repetition before a theme outstays

Sketches for the fourth movement of the Piano Sonata in B-flat, op. 106 ("Hammerklavier"). A single, simple rising figure dominates the entire page. *Library of Congress*

its welcome. (This is one of the reasons why the typical popular song is so much shorter than the typical movement of instrumental music.) How, then, to sustain and develop an initial idea? Like his immediate models Mozart and Haydn, and like countless other composers before them, Beethoven drew on two basic techniques over and over again: variation and counterpoint.

To vary a melody or motif is to alter it in such a way that it retains some vestige of the original idea and yet is distinctly different from it. The opening of the Fifth Symphony is a paradigm of variation technique. The first four notes are instantly recognizable because of their rhythm and their pitches: three quick iterations of the note G followed by a longer E-flat. This creates the distinctive short-short-short-LONG rhythm we will hear so often in this movement. There is no harmony here at first, for all the instruments play in unison. This is the idea to be varied.

Beethoven begins to manipulate this idea at once. He repeats it right away with the same rhythm, the same orchestration, and the same dynamics (loud), but now down a step: instead of three Gs going to E-flat we hear three Fs going to D. And now the changes begin to come faster and faster. After a long pause on D, the music becomes very soft, and the simple unison texture gives way to a rapid-fire dialogue among the stringed instruments, which toss the basic idea back and forth, altering the pitches and intervals slightly each time. But the rhythm remains constant. It is this kind of intense variation that makes the opening of the Fifth Symphony so gripping. The music is at once both simple and complex, straightforward and subtle. And it all goes by in just a few seconds.

Counterpoint is the other basic technique by which to sustain and elaborate a theme. It involves juxtaposing an additional line or lines against a given idea. Counterpoint always involves multiple layers of forward motion: ideally, each line is substantive in its own right and able to stand on its own even as it blends seamlessly with all the others. A demanding art, counterpoint was for centuries the touchstone of compositional ability. Harmony, by contrast, was considered not nearly so difficult. Anyone with a bit of training, so the thinking went, could provide a series of underlying chords to a given line of melody. But to create multiple pleasing lines of equal weight that could function independently and at the same time complement each other was a challenge of an altogether different magnitude.

Beethoven learned counterpoint the way it had been taught for centuries, which happens to be the way it is still taught today. His exercises with Haydn, Johann Georg Albrechtsberger, and Antonio Salieri (of *Amadeus* fame) thus look very familiar to the trained eye: the instructor gives a *cantus firmus*—a "firm" or "fixed" melodic line—and the pupil writes additional lines above it, below it, or both. The exercise progresses from simple note-against-note

counterpoint in two voices to more elaborate and rhythmically complicated layers of three, four, or even five additional voices. The challenge is to create new lines around the *cantus firmus* that carry their
own distinctive melodic profiles and do not merely shadow the contour of any other voice, all the while avoiding unwanted dissonance,
parallel motion at the interval of a fifth between voices, and a host of
other technical no-nos.

When Beethoven's teachers corrected these exercises in counterpoint, they were not addressing mistakes so much as suggesting
better alternatives. These usually involved creating more interesting melodic lines or more contrast between the directions of
different voices. And while these exercises give the appearance of
being just that—dry exercises, not real music—they in fact instilled
techniques that would become second nature to Beethoven and
that surface constantly in his finished works. We can hear one particularly clear example of this in the finale of the Ninth Symphony
when the "Ode to Joy" theme returns and is juxtaposed against the
contrasting theme associated with the words "Seid umschlungen,
Millionen!" ("Be embraced, ye millions!"). This is counterpoint at
its finest, with two distinctly different melodies running in tandem.
To make things even more intricate, Beethoven has each of these
themes enter against itself at staggered temporal intervals in other
voices. This latter device, known as imitative counterpoint, is basic
to canons and fugues. Each voice is more or less the same as the
others, but they enter in succession: "Row, Row, Row Your Boat"
and "Frère Jacques," for example, are canons, the strictest form of
imitative counterpoint, because all the voices are exactly the same.
In a fugue, the individual voices are very similar but not identical,
and the imitation can give way at times to passages that are free of
imitation altogether.

Having invented and elaborated a musical idea using the
techniques of variation and counterpoint, Beethoven's next task
was to expand and integrate the constructed passage into a larger
whole. The principles of musical form are really quite simple. Having

stated an idea of any length—call it "A"—a composer has only three choices as to what to do next: repeat it (A), vary it (A'), or contrast it against a different idea (B). All musical forms are based on some combination of these three moves.

Beethoven drew on a number of inherited large-scale formal conventions. The simplest of these was theme and variations, in which a theme is varied in a series of discrete, modular units (Theme, Variation 1, Variation 2, etc.). Beethoven wrote variation sets throughout his life, either as stand-alone works or as movements within a larger cycle such as a sonata, string quartet, or symphony. He cultivated the form with particular intensity in his early years, in part because variations sold well in the sheet music marketplace, in part because the form allowed him to hone his craft within a clearly structured framework.

Another conventional form of Beethoven's time was the rondo, so called because it derived from the "round" dance of that name. Here, variation (A A') and contrast (A B) work in tandem. The opening theme—typically short and catchy—keeps returning in a slightly varied form, but only after we have heard contrasting ideas. The pattern, then, could manifest itself as something like A B A' C A'' B' A'''. The rondo was a favorite form for finales, as in the Violin Concerto, the Triple Concerto (for violin, cello, and piano), or the "Pathétique" Sonata for Piano, op. 13.

Predictability is an important feature of all conventional forms and especially in purely instrumental music, where listeners have no text by which to follow the course of the music. The two most widely used large-scale formal conventions in Beethoven's time were binary form and sonata form.

Like the rondo, binary form—so-called because it consists of two sections—originated in the world of dance. Dance music of all kinds is typically full of large-scale repetitions, and in binary form the first section is normally repeated before moving on to the second section, which also repeats. In sonatas, string quartets, symphonies, and the like, binary forms could be used as modular building blocks.

This is especially common in minuet or scherzo movements. The first binary form, is followed by a contrasting binary form, known as the trio, after which the first binary form is repeated *da capo*—literally "from the head," or as we would say more colloquially, "from the top." We find this pattern repeatedly in Beethoven's minuets and scherzos, sometimes with additional trios, as in the Seventh and Ninth Symphonies. The structural principle in each case is modular. And not everything is completely predictable: toward the end of the scherzos in both the Seventh and Ninth Symphonies, what sounds like yet another return of the trio section is abruptly cut off shortly after it begins. Beethoven knew how to play with listeners' expectations.

What would later come to be called sonata form—the most common form for the first movement of any large-scale instrumental work in Beethoven's time—is in effect an extension of binary form. It, too, consists of two halves. The first is the exposition, in which the movement's principal melodic ideas are introduced ("exposed") in the tonic or "home" key. One or more contrasting themes are then introduced in a different but closely related key. This move to a new key area, known as modulation, keeps the music fresh. (This is why church organists often modulate just before the last verse of a hymn, lifting the music up a notch. If everything remained in the same key throughout, it would all begin to sound just a bit tired.)

The second half of a sonata-form movement falls into two subsections. The first is the development, in which the themes heard in the exposition are varied, often in fragmented form. This section scrupulously avoids the tonic so that when we return to the home key, we feel a strong sense of return, a sense that we have been here before—which in fact we have. The reiteration of the tonic is typically reinforced by a simultaneous return to the opening theme. This moment marks the beginning of the recapitulation, the second subsection of the movement's second half. Here, the themes we had heard in the related key in the exposition are now transposed to the tonic. Sonata-form movements could open with a slow introduction before the beginning of the exposition, and they could conclude with a coda (Italian for "tail") after the end of the recapitulation, but these are optional elements that stand outside the basic structure of sonata form itself.

Sonata form was a template, not a mold, and composers were free to take liberties within this very broad outline. This scheme worked to the benefit of composers and listeners alike. It gave composers a framework for the large-scale presentation and elaboration of multiple ideas, and it gave listeners a framework of expectations about how a movement's musical events would unfold. In this sense, sonata form is a way of telling a musical story in which the themes are analogous to characters, while the key areas can be thought of as locations. We get to know the characters (themes) on their home turf in the exposition, they experience things away from home in the development, and there is a resolution of some kind when they return home in the recapitulation. This pattern—home, away from home, back home—is basic to a great many stories, both verbal and musical.

We can think of *The Wizard of Oz*, for example, in terms of sonata form. We meet all the characters in the exposition either on the farm (Dorothy, Hunk, Hickory, Zeke, Miss Gulch) or not too far away from the farm soon after Dorothy runs away (Professor Marvel). Transported to Oz—the development section—the characters take on new but still recognizable forms: the farmhands morph into the Scarecrow, the Tin Woodsman, and the Cowardly Lion; Miss Gulch becomes the Wicked Witch of the West, and Professor Marvel becomes the Wizard. Back in Kansas at the end—the recapitulation—all the characters (save Miss Gulch) reappear in their original form. Even Professor Marvel, whom we had not seen on the farm (the tonic) when we first met him but only away from it (in the related key area), is now incorporated into the "home" key. As in a sonata-form movement, we see the characters—or hear the themes—in a new light when we encounter them again in the recapitulation. They are the same but not the same.

Sonata form allows for countless permutations even while remaining recognizable in its general outlines. In Beethoven's Fifth Symphony, for example, we hear something quite startling and unexpected about two-thirds of the way through the first movement. The return of the opening theme in the tonic tells us that the recapitulation has begun, but the music suddenly comes to a halt and we hear a solo oboe playing a new, mournful theme entirely by itself. The rest of the orchestra falls silent for a brief and highly dramatic moment. This goes against all conventions of sonata form and makes its effect in part for just this reason: we simply do not expect this sort of thing to happen. At the same time, we can still apprehend the larger shape of the movement when the orchestra interrupts the oboe and the recapitulation resumes its expected course. Our experience with the conventions of sonata form enhances the sense of surprise even while confirming a larger sense of structure once the recapitulation resumes its expected course.

There was, however, one important genre during Beethoven's lifetime for which listeners could entertain no expectations of any kind: the fantasia. Often improvised at the keyboard and only occasionally committed to paper, fantasias were perceived as the unmediated product of the imagination or "fantasy" of the performer-composer, produced spontaneously and without reflection in what we today would call a stream-of-consciousness fashion. When critics of Beethoven's time described the fantasia as a genre with "no theme," they meant that it had no *central* theme that listeners could reasonably expect to be manipulated and then brought back at some point. The title "fantasia" was in effect a warning label: abandon all expectations, ye who listen here.

Beethoven was renowned for his abilities to fantasize at the keyboard. Indeed, the occasional concerts he organized typically included an extended solo improvisation. He committed only two of these fantasias to paper, one for piano (the Fantasia, op. 77), the other for an ensemble of piano, orchestra, vocal soloists, and chorus (the Choral Fantasy, op. 80). Neither adheres to any formal convention. Both open with broad flourishes on the piano and move through a variety of moods and fragmentary ideas before landing on a theme that becomes the basis of further variation and improvisation. About midway through the Choral Fantasy, Beethoven brings in an orchestra that together with the piano elaborates the "discovered" melody still further. The piece concludes with solo voices and chorus declaiming a text on the power of art.

Fantasy was equated with inspiration, that magical moment of invention. And Beethoven's contemporaries, including even his detractors, consistently lauded his fantasy. But his detractors accused him of putting it on display to excess: they regarded too much fantasy as detrimental to any composition not labeled as such. Critics recognized the free play of imagination as a necessary starting point for the invention of ideas but always hastened to add that subjective fantasy needed to be tempered by objective circumspection. Otherwise, a composer's spontaneous ideas ran the risk of becoming incomprehensible. When an early critic called the "Eroica" Symphony an extended fantasy for orchestra, it was not meant as a compliment.[4]

We have much to learn from critics like this. They remind us that Beethoven challenged the listeners of his time, and that listeners were not used to being challenged. Music criticism would take a new turn in the generation that followed, with the benefit of the doubt going to composers. But this was a new way of listening that had not yet established itself in Beethoven's day.

Regardless of genre, the next step in the composition of any new work was to supervise the process of publication. This was a time-consuming and vexatious task, one Beethoven loathed but accepted as a necessary evil. He reviewed and corrected proofs of the publisher's score, often berating engravers for their mistakes.

Nor was the process necessarily over once a publisher had issued a work. Beethoven lived at a time when new technologies were beginning to allow composers to indicate exactly how fast their music should be performed. Generations of his predecessors had made do with fairly broad designations, usually in Italian, that designated a mood as much as a speed, such as *Allegro* (lively, fast), *Presto* (very fast), *Andante* (a walking pace), *Adagio* (slow), or *Lento* (very slow). But how fast is fast? How slow is slow? Johann Nepomuk Mälzel, a personal friend of the composer, helped perfect the metronome, a new device that could measure beats per minute with a fair degree of exactitude. Beethoven liked the idea and proceeded to add metronome markings to at least some of his works already in circulation, including his first eight symphonies and a number of string quartets. Oddly, he provided markings for only one of his piano sonatas, op. 106 ("Hammerklavier"), and these strike many performers today as impossibly fast. Other metronome indications have come down through the memory of his pupil and associate Carl Czerny.

But original editions, even those approved and revised by the composer, are still not the last word. Mistakes, ambiguities, inconsistencies, and conflicting readings among relevant sources have generated the need for carefully edited modern editions. Scholars today are now in the process of producing a complete set of Beethoven's works that reconciles such discrepancies. The most recent edition of the Fifth Symphony, for example, is based on a variety of different and often conflicting sources, the most important of which are the composer's autograph score (itself full of Beethoven's own corrections and additions); the set of parts used for the first performance, also with Beethoven's corrections and changes; a copyist's manuscript of the score, again with similar changes in the composer's hand; correspondence with Breitkopf & Härtel, the original publisher; and the first publication itself, issued in orchestral parts in April 1809.[5] Weighing all these sources against each other is a painstaking process, but the end result is a score that reflects the composer's intentions as can best be determined. Beethoven would no doubt be amazed—and gratified—by the care with which such editions are made today.

Chapter 9

Early—Middle—Late

Critics and historians have long divided Beethoven's music into three stylistic periods—early, middle, and late—in an attempt to trace the trajectory of his output in its broadest terms. This tripartite scheme has its advantages and limitations, for it shapes how we hear the music in ways that are sometimes helpful, sometimes not.

The dividing lines that separate the three periods have varied considerably over the years. This in itself is a good reminder of their inherently arbitrary nature. The consensus nowadays aligns them with two major moments of crisis in the composer's life, the first coinciding with the Heiligenstadt Testament (late 1802), the second with the end of the affair with the Immortal Beloved (late 1812), which led to a temporary decline in both the quantity and quality of music produced over the next two years. It was around 1815 that Beethoven seems to have found renewed energy and began to write in what is now considered his "late" style.[1]

In the world of the arts, a tripartite division of this kind is scarcely unique to Beethoven, for it reflects a stock progression from youth (learning) to maturity (full powers) to old age (transcendence or decline). In terms of style, commentators generally delineate Beethoven's three periods as follows:

Beethoven's Three Style Periods and the Major Genres

Genres	Early (through 1802)	Middle (1803-15)	Late (1815-27)
Symphonies	nos. 1 and 2	nos. 3–8	no. 9
Piano Sonatas	op. 2–28	op. 31–90	opp. 101–111
String Quartets	op. 18	opp. 59, 74, 95	opp. 127, 130, 131, 132, 135

Early: The works of the early period are often characterized as following in the tradition of Haydn and Mozart. This is true, but only up to a point. Like any aspiring composer, Beethoven looked to acknowledged masters for his models, and he cultivated the formal and harmonic language of what is often called the "Classical style." But audiences recognized Haydn and Mozart in their own time as brilliantly original and unpredictable, sometimes too much so. Some of Mozart's string quartets, as one critic complained in the 1780s, were "too highly seasoned." This tradition of novelty was an important part of what Beethoven assimilated in his early years in Vienna. It would be grossly mistaken to regard such works as the Piano Sonata op. 13 ("Pathétique") or the Sonatas op. 27, nos. 1 and 2 ("Moonlight"), or the Second Symphony as mere imitations of earlier composers' styles. We hear already in these works an original voice that is unquestionably different from that of any predecessor.

Middle: Critics typically regard the works of the middle period as quintessentially Beethovenian, for they reflect the composer's move beyond the "early" style but do not yet bear the distinctive (and for some, problematic) elements of the "late" style. Many of the best-known works of this period are characterized as "heroic" on the grounds that they are monumental in both scale and tone and often convey a sense of struggle and resolution, as in the Fifth Symphony, whose stormy C-minor opening movement culminates in a triumphant C-major finale. The "Eroica" Symphony is longer than even the longest works in the same genre by Haydn or Mozart (or even by Beethoven himself) by a ratio of almost 2:1. The same holds for the first of the three String Quartets of op. 59 and the Fifth Piano Concerto, op. 73 ("Emperor").

Late: The "late" works are often perceived to reflect Beethoven's increasing isolation from society during the last decade of his life. Critics hear a heightened degree of introspection in this music, particularly when compared against the "heroic" works of the previous decade. (The Ninth Symphony is a notable exception.) Works of the late style adopt radically new forms and explore extremes of dimensions: the Quartet in C-sharp minor, op. 131, for example, opens with an extended fugue instead of the expected movement in sonata form and consists of seven movements rather than the usual four. Two of these movements, moreover, are extremely brief. Beyond this, Beethoven calls for all seven movements to be played in one continuous sequence, without any breaks between them. Here and in other late works, the tone is also different: at times it is difficult to tell whether Beethoven intends for us to take particular passages seriously or as a joke—or as both at once. The fifth-movement scherzo of op. 131, for example, features moments at which the unsuspecting listener would swear the cellist has entered too early, though this is in fact not the case. The music sounds "wrong" on purpose.

For all the necessary caveats, there is ample musical evidence to support this broad construct of three periods. The string quartets, represented roughly equally in each of the three periods (six early, five middle, five late), provide a good basis of comparison. If we begin with the extremes, we can see obvious differences between the early and late works of this genre. The six quartets of op. 18 follow the standard four-movement format inherited from Haydn and Mozart and stay squarely within the conventional harmonic idiom of the day. Indeed, there is nothing in opus 18 as harmonically daring as the slow introduction to Mozart's "Dissonance" Quartet in C Major,

K. 465, though Beethoven makes an attempt in that direction in the finale of op. 18, no. 6, marked "La malinconia" ("Melancholy"). In terms of the formal design of individual movements, moreover, Haydn's op. 76 quartets (published 1799) are on the whole far more unconventional than Beethoven's op. 18 quartets. The first movement of op. 76, no. 5, defies all formal categories, and its deeply moving slow movement, marked "Largo: Cantabile e mesto" ("Extremely slow: lyrical and sad") is in the remarkable key of F-sharp major. The second-movement "Fantasia" of op. 76, no. 6, in turn, includes daring modulations, and the first movement of the same work presents a set of variations in which the theme itself scarcely changes, only the voices around it.

Beethoven's op. 59 string quartets of 1808, on the other hand, occupy a very different musical world. The first of the three in this set is the chamber-music counterpart to the "Eroica" Symphony, with a first movement of unprecedented dimension and textural complexity. Like the "Eroica," it incorporates a fugato—an extended section with thematic imitation between the voices, in the manner of a fugue—and an overarching sense of struggle that culminates in a triumphal restatement of what at first had seemed to be a relatively modest opening theme. The middle-period quartets also make technical demands of a kind string players had rarely if ever encountered. Opus 74 (known as the "Harp" because of the repeated plucking figures in the first movement) includes devilishly difficult passages not only for the first violinist but for the three other players as well. And musicians who follow the composer's metronome marking for the fugue that concludes op. 59, no. 3, face considerable challenges indeed.

If the middle-period string quartets occupy a different musical world, the late ones—opp. 127, 130, 131, 132, 135—take us to the edge of a different universe. Two of them (opp. 127 and 135) conform to the standard four-movement pattern but the other three follow trajectories that are completely sui generis. And even the four-movement works are unconventional in their own way. Critics have often described the opening movement of op. 127, for example, as "floating": the music moves back and forth between a bold, fanfare-like figure and a lyrical theme, and the movement as a whole lacks the forward drive so typical of middle-period works. The texture is also profoundly polyphonic, with an unprecedented independence among the voices: this, too, is a typical feature of late-style works. In one of the conversation books, Beethoven's brother Johann tells the composer after one performance of the work that the "interweaving" of the four instruments "is so rich that one is fully occupied just observing a single voice; therefore each [listener] wished that he could hear the quartet four times."[2]

The six-movement String Quartet, op. 130, is even more uncon-ventional. Its opening movement has a start-and-stop quality still more pronounced than in its counterpart in op. 127, and when the music first moves away from the tonic of B-flat major for the first time, it overshoots the expected key of F and lands instead on G-flat. Even those who think they might not be able to discern such an unconventional move will sense that something is slightly "off" at this point. The second-movement scherzo goes by so quickly—it typically runs under two minutes in performance—that its ab-rupt ending comes as a surprise. More extraordinary still is the fifth movement, marked "Cavatina," a term that up to this point had been reserved for small-scale arias of an introspective character. Introspective, indeed: in simulating a soprano overcome by tears, the first violin seems to gasp for breath at one point. Beethoven marks the passage *beklemmt*, literally "caught in a vise," and the melody, when performed this way, sounds very much like that of an oper-atic heroine who is so emotionally devastated that she is gasping for breath, unable to project her voice in all its fullness. Here the com-poser asks for dramatic realism in place of beauty; violinists, trained to create beautiful tone, often struggle to make the moment sound as labored as it should. This kind of raw, realistic emotion was some-thing new in instrumental music. Beauty was no longer the primary consideration.

And then we come to the finale, which is perhaps the essence of the late style. Instead of the sense of inevitability so often perceived in the "heroic" works of the middle period, the performers have a choice of two entirely different endings. The original finale is an enormous fugue, substantially longer than any of the quartet's previous movements. Critics have likened it to J. S. Bach's *The Art of Fugue* because of its almost encyclopedic application of contrapuntal devices, some of them quite arcane. Beethoven called it *tantôt libre, tantôt recherchée*, at times free, at times *recherchée* in the full sense of that word: "researched," artificial, arcane, obscure. This movement (later published separately as the *Grosse Fuge* or "Great Fugue," op. 133) can be as exhausting to listen to as it is to perform. When the publisher Artaria suggested that Beethoven write a different finale—and offered him an additional sum—the composer agreed, in part because he too must have recognized that the fugal finale threatened to overwhelm the rest of the work. But he had known full well what he was doing when he had written the original finale, and the publisher's offer gave him the opportunity to demonstrate that two completely different endings to the same work could be equally satisfying, each in its own way. The substitute finale is a light, lively, and much shorter movement, one filled with the rhythms of a country dance. Which is better? Fortunately, we do not have to decide: quartets today perform the work both ways, sometimes with the original fugue, sometimes with the substitute finale.

In short, the late style is characterized by an exploration of musical extremes of dimension and proportion (very long and very short movements juxtaposed), of texture (with a particular emphasis on counterpoint and especially fugue), of harmony (both local and long-range), and of tone (serious or playful or both at the same time).

The Early—Middle—Late division is not without its problems, however. Each of these periods is a construct, an imagined category that does not always align with the works of the period in question. Critics have from time to time modified these lines of demarcation, proposing additional style-periods or subdivisions of the standard three. But even these modifications cannot explain away a late work like the Ninth Symphony, in which Beethoven reverts to the "heroic" tone of his middle period, in which struggle leads to a moment of crisis (at the beginning of the finale) and resolution (with the introduction of voices and the "Ode to Joy" theme). Yet to say that it "reverts" is to suggest that the work represents a backward step, which in a hundred other ways it most assuredly does not.

The tripartite scheme also shapes the way we hear the music, and not always to its (or our) advantage. In the case of the early period in particular, we are inclined to listen—probably unconsciously—to what these works are *not*: not yet the fate-by-the-throat-grabbing Beethoven, not yet the product of a composer determined to go his own way, convention be damned. His contemporaries heard this music quite differently. One early reviewer of the Piano Trios op. 1 (1795) expressed regret that "out of an evident desire to be entirely new, Beethoven is not infrequently incomprehensible, incoherent, and opaque." Another critic, reviewing the Violin Sonatas op. 12 (1798), decried the composer's "bizarre," "overly learned," and "arduous" manner of writing.[3] These are works written supposedly in the shadow of Mozart and Haydn, yet the vocabulary used to describe them when they first appeared is no different from that which critics would be using a quarter century later in talking about works of the late period. Ears change.

The construct of the middle period, in turn, implicitly encourages the idea that there is a "real" Beethoven, a central core to the body of his work. This reinforces the inclination to hear the early works as not yet fully developed and the late ones as deviations from a supposed standard. The image of the "heroic Beethoven" rests on a remarkably small number of works from the middle period: the Third and Fifth Symphonies, the third *Leonore* overture, *Fidelio*, the Piano Concertos 4 and 5, and a handful of sonatas.[4] Works like the Fourth and Eighth Symphonies and the Piano Sonatas opp. 54, 78, and 79 are often described in the same misleading terms as the Ninth, as "reversions." But these supposed reversions are more than sufficient to undermine the validity of an imagined teleological trajectory.

To regard Beethoven's output as the manifestation of some enormous Hegelian dialectic, with each previous work canceled out and absorbed into the next, is to imagine the composer's life as moving in a straight and inexorable line. This ignores Beethoven's enduring and fundamental tendency to adopt multiple perspectives toward whatever task lay at hand. When Karl Holz asked him which of the three "Galitzin" String Quartets (opp. 127, 130, 132) was the greatest, he reported Beethoven's response thus: "Each in its own way! Art demands of us that we not stand still."[5] But not standing still is not the same as always moving forward in a single direction. For Beethoven, it more typically meant circling around an object— music—to assume an ever-widening series of perspectives.

Chapter 10

The Music

Beethoven wrote in virtually every genre of his time: symphonies, concertos, overtures, sonatas of all kinds, trios, quartets, quintets, and larger chamber ensembles, songs, oratorio, opera, and sacred music. Listeners today enjoy easy access to program notes that describe individual works in detail.

Broader perspectives that transcend specific works can help us understand the music at a still deeper level. Even something as seemingly simple as the way in which Beethoven numbered his own works, for example, has much to tell us about the composer's perception of what he wrote. Although he had published a fair number of pieces by the middle of the 1790s, he waited quite deliberately before conferring the portentous designation "Opus 1" on anything he had written. The label "opus" (Latin for "work," abbreviated as "op.") carried real weight, and the three piano trios of op. 1, issued in July 1795, are easily his most substantial pieces to that point, large four-movement works dedicated to his principal patron at the time, Prince Lichnowsky. Beethoven then waited another nine months before releasing anything he considered worthy of bearing the label op. 2. This was an equally weighty collection of three piano sonatas

dedicated to his teacher Joseph Haydn. In the meantime, he had
continued to issue further small-scale works without opus numbers,
mostly piano variations and orchestral dances. This pattern would
continue throughout his life: works designated by opus numbers
interspersed with what he considered lesser ones, to which scholars
have since assigned arbitrary "WoO" numbers, short for *Werke ohne
Opuszahl* ("Works without Opus Numbers").

These works without opus numbers are by no means necessarily of lesser quality, however. The set of Twelve Variations for
Piano and Cello, WoO 45, on the chorus "See the Conqu'ring Hero
Comes" from Handel's oratorio *Judas Maccabaeus*, for example, is
every bit the equal of later variations issued with opus numbers,
in terms both of scale and of the demands it makes on performers.
Published by Artaria of Vienna in 1797, it is dedicated to Princess
Maria Christiane von Lichnowsky, the wife of the same patron to
whom Beethoven had dedicated the Piano Trios op. 1. Why no opus
number, then? Variations were regarded as a genre of lesser prestige
than sonatas or piano trios. Not until 1803, with the piano variations op. 34 and op. 35, did Beethoven issue a set of variations with
an opus number. These were on themes of his own invention, and
in a letter to Breitkopf of December 1802 he called attention to
his desire to release each of these two sets with a "proper number
within *my greater musical works*."[1] Beethoven was in fact one of the
first composers to exert a reasonable control over the numbering of
his own works, so that with occasional exceptions an opus number
reflects a given composition's date of publication.

But what did these works *mean*? Did they in fact mean anything
at all? Or as one anonymous critic asked in the summer of 1827,
just a few months after Beethoven's death, "Should one think about
something while listening to instrumental music?"[2] These are age-
old questions, and they still resonate today. Listeners have always
been able to relate a work of vocal music to the text being sung,
but hearing music that has no words of any sort and whose title is

literally generic (Symphony no. 2, Sonata in C Major, etc.) creates a
different kind of challenge.

Beethoven himself had to walk a fine line on this point. On the
one hand, he gave descriptive titles to at least some of his instrumental works, such as the "Eroica" and the "Pastoral" symphonies,
the "Pathétique" and "Les Adieux" piano sonatas. At times he even
went so far as to give individual movements their own titles, as in the
"Funeral March" (the second movement of the "Eroica" Symphony),
the "Funeral March on the Death of a Hero" (the second movement of the Piano Sonata op. 26), and "The Awakening of Happy
Feelings upon Arriving in the Countryside" (the first movement of
the "Pastoral" Symphony). On the other hand, he felt it necessary
to point out that the "Pastoral" was "more the expression of feeling
than tone-painting."[3] He knew that critics had long regarded tone-
painting—the depiction of real-world sounds through music, such
as battles, frogs croaking, or birds singing—as music of a lower
order, but oddly enough, and in the "Pastoral" no less, he took pains
to identify the species of bird calls presented toward the end of its
second movement: nightingale, cuckoo, and quail. Listeners were
sometimes forgiving in such instances, sometimes not. They greeted
Wellington's Victory enthusiastically at first, no doubt because of
the wave of patriotism sweeping Austria at the time, but many of
them later found the same work embarrassing, precisely because the
depictions of cannon and musket fire left so little to the imagination.

Still, clues to what works might be "about" were always welcome,
even if they were secondhand. The composer's alleged description of
the opening of the Fifth Symphony as "fate pounding at the portal,"
for example, came from the unreliable Anton Schindler long after
the fact. Schindler also reported that the composer had connected
the Piano Sonata in D minor, op. 31, no. 2, with Shakespeare's play
The Tempest. We cannot dismiss such testimony out of hand. The
more reliable Ferdinand Ries recalled that his teacher "frequently
had a certain subject in mind when he composed," and his fellow
pupil Czerny suggested as much as well. The sketches occasionally

confirm such an approach. An early draft for the String Quartet in F Major, op. 18, no. 1, for example, shows that Beethoven was thinking of the tomb scene of Shakespeare's *Romeo and Juliet* while composing the slow movement, which he marked "Adagio affettuoso ed appassionato" ("Slowly, with loving feeling and passionately").[4] In the end, however, Beethoven rarely gave clues about what images or stories might have inspired him.

The dramatic nature of so many of the composer's best-known works has certainly tempted many listeners to create narratives of their own that match the music. The wordless marital spat between Sid Caesar and Nanette Fabray in a December 1954 airing of the television variety show *Caesar's Hour*, played against the first movement of the Fifth Symphony, is both hilarious and revealing. Gestures, facial expressions, and body language suffice; no words are needed. At the very beginning, we see a close-up of opposing accusatory hands thrust forward against the famous opening motif: first his, then hers. The camera pans out and the pace picks up: we see a brief moment of reconciliation with the entrance of the lyrical theme in E-flat major; recriminations resume with the development; energy flags toward the end of the development, followed by the most vehement recriminations of all at the beginning of the recapitulation. One last, futile effort at forgiveness is mimed against the plaintive, unexpected oboe solo but then abandoned when the orchestra resumes full-throttle. The skit concludes with a final resolution to the sound of the march-like theme that closes out the movement. The two comedians have tapped brilliantly into the essentially dramatic nature of the music. Is this movement about a marital spat? Of course not. But it is about conflict of some kind.

The sticking point is always the degree of specificity. In a widely discussed essay first published in 1985, the music historian Owen Jander proposed that the middle movement of the Fourth Piano Concerto depicts Orpheus in the Underworld pleading his case before Pluto and Proserpina for the return of his beloved Eurydice. In Jander's reading, the harsh, angular outbursts of the orchestra

W. J. Mähler's portrait from 1804 or 1805 depicts Beethoven as an Orpheus-like figure, moving from darkness to light, perhaps in the process of turning around to see if his Eurydice is indeed behind him. The instrument he holds is a lyre-guitar, a fashionable instrument of the time that reinforces the image of a modern-day Orpheus. *Wien Museum*

represent the gods of the Underworld, while Orpheus makes his case with the piano, a simulacrum of the mythic figure's lyre. The two engage in dialogue, and the orchestra's wrath gradually subsides, mirroring (Jander argues) the process by which the gods fall into a trance. After a passage of high tension—repeated trills and runs in the piano—we hear a moment of miraculous transformation as Orpheus, still alive, passes into the realm of the dead.[5] Beethoven's own representation of himself as Orpheus in Mähler's portrait of him gives further support to this reading.

Even those who reject the specificity of Jander's scenario concede that the orchestra and piano are engaged in a dialogue of some sort and that the piano, in its own pleading way, eventually wins out by subduing the orchestra. But is the music really "about" this specific situation? Or is it only about itself, which is to say the play of opposing musical forces? Reasonable minds continue to disagree on this point.

Titles can tell us something even when they are literally generic (symphony, string quartet, sonata, etc.). They identify and allow us to anticipate not only the performance forces of the work at hand but also its general formal outline. A symphony, for example, is a work for full orchestra and typically consists of four movements: a fast first movement in sonata form, a slow movement in a different key, a lively minuet or scherzo movement in the tonic in triple meter (three beats to the measure), and a fast finale, most often in rondo or sonata form. The same pattern holds for many genres of chamber music (with only player per part) and piano sonatas, though the minuet/scherzo movement is sometimes absent from these. These conventions are by no means immutable: the "Pastoral" Symphony consists of five movements, and the Ninth incorporates vocal soloists and a chorus into its finale.

Yet even these exceptions operate within a still broader convention of what might be called a genre's tone. For Beethoven's generation and well beyond, the symphony was the most prestigious of all instrumental genres, the one in which composers could most readily demonstrate their command of orchestration and large-scale form. It was also among the least commercially attractive. Consumers who would readily buy piano and chamber music were not in the market for works that required an ensemble of forty or more players. They might purchase arrangements of symphonies, most commonly for piano, piano duo (four-hands), or piano trio (piano, violin, and cello), but not the original works themselves.

That Beethoven wrote as many symphonies as he did is in itself remarkable, given the changing nature of the musical scene in Vienna at the time. Whereas Haydn had written more than a hundred of them, mostly for his orchestra at the Esterházy court, and then later for Paris and London, Beethoven had no orchestra readily at his disposal. In 1800, the year of his First Symphony, Vienna could offer very few truly public concerts, that is, concerts open to anyone who could afford a ticket of admission. Even these were mostly ad hoc affairs: there was no standing civic orchestra, and regular concert series would not appear on the scene for another decade or more. (In a revealing coincidence, the Vienna Philharmonic and the New York Philharmonic were both founded in the same year, 1842.)

There is no quintessential Beethoven symphony: each has its own distinct profile, especially from the Third onward. The "Eroica" is truly revolutionary, not only because of its sheer size but also because of its structural complexity, its sonorities, the weight of its finale, and what might be called its ethical dimension: it wrestles with the ideas of heroism, struggle, death, and victory. Even without the subtitle ("Heroic Symphony") and the (canceled) dedication to Napoleon, listeners of the time would have readily recognized the first movement's opening theme as a military-style horn call and the second movement as a funeral march. The latter raises issues of life and death in a genre that until then had been perceived largely as a vehicle of entertainment, not of moral or philosophical ideas. But the simulated sound of muffled drums at the beginning of the march and the gradual slowing-down of the clock-like rhythm toward the end combine to remind us of human mortality. With the "Eroica," instrumental music in general and the symphony in particular began to move beyond the realm of mere pleasure.

From a more technical perspective, Beethoven's innovations in the formal design of his symphonies extend from the level of the individual movement to the cycle as a whole. His addition of vocal soloists and chorus in the finale of the Ninth Symphony is merely the most striking of the many ways in which he explored fundamentally new approaches to the genre. Again, he liked to look at a single object—in this case, the genre of the symphony—from multiple perspectives. The Fourth features a slow introduction of unprecedented gravity and length, offset by a rollicking first movement that gives extraordinary prominence to the tympani. In this work, Beethoven also began to explore in depth the possibility of linking all four movements through a particular intervallic motive (B-flat to G-flat). He would take up this same challenge in a different way in the Fifth Symphony, which explores ways of linking all four movements through the transformation of a prominent rhythmic motive (short-short-short-LONG) and through the return of one movement (the third) within the course of another (the fourth).

The Sixth ("Pastoral") Symphony is an example of what has come to be known as "program music," instrumental music that seeks to convey ideas, images, or events through sound with the aid of a descriptive title, movement titles, or a more elaborate prose "program." The Seventh, perhaps the most popular of all Beethoven's symphonies during the nineteenth century, eschews programmatic headings but explores the element of rhythm with unparalleled intensity: Richard Wagner would later call it the "Apotheosis of Dance."[6] The Eighth, often overshadowed by its larger siblings, is a biting essay in humor and irony. The Ninth, in turn, raised symphonic monumentality to unprecedented heights, both in its length and in its incorporation of sung text in its finale. This was a move that would spark tremendous controversy in the decades that followed, but even detractors agreed that after Beethoven, the symphony was a fundamentally new genre. Composers could now, in effect, philosophize in music.

In addition to symphonies, Beethoven wrote about a dozen single-movement works for orchestra. Some of these (*Egmont, King Stephen, Ruins of Athens, Consecration of the House*) were overtures to spoken dramas for which he wrote incidental music as well. Others (*Coriolanus, Name-Day*) were written expressly for the concert hall, with no opera or drama to follow. Beethoven ultimately rejected the three overtures to the opera *Leonore* in favor of the one for the renamed *Fidelio*; the third of the *Leonore* overtures (op. 72b) would become a standalone favorite in the concert hall. With the exception of the *Name-Day* overture, op. 115 (originally conceived as "an overture for any occasion or for use in a concert"), all of these works reflect in some way the emotional worlds of the dramas with which they are connected. In this way, they are important forerunners of the "symphonic poems" or "tone poems" by such later composers as Franz Liszt and Richard Strauss.

But it was through the piano that Beethoven established his reputation, and the piano concerto was the ideal vehicle for him to showcase his talents both as a composer and performer. By the premiere of the last of the five in 1811, however, growing deafness had forced him to cede the role of soloist to his student, Archduke Rudolph. In this same work (later nicknamed the "Emperor" Concerto because of its size and grandeur), Beethoven broke with convention in the first movement by instructing the soloist to play a written-out cadenza rather than the expected improvisation of the performer's own making. The Violin Concerto, in turn, remains a staple of the repertory, as does the Triple Concerto for piano, violin, cello, and orchestra.

The thirty-two piano sonatas are central to the solo repertory of that instrument and span the whole of Beethoven's career. Like the symphonies, they explore an astonishing variety of styles. Most are in three or four movements, some in only two. With only a few exceptions, all are far more technically demanding than what was customary at the time; this undoubtedly cut into sales and helped foster Beethoven's reputation as a "difficult" composer. The "late" sonatas (opp. 101, 106, 109, 110, 111) are especially challenging. Opus 106 (nicknamed the "Hammerklavier") has been called the "Mount Everest of the Piano" because of its size and technical difficulty, particularly its fugal finale.

Although overshadowed by the piano sonatas to some extent, the ten sonatas for violin and piano and the five sonatas for cello and piano are every bit as ambitious and wide-ranging. The "Kreutzer" Sonata for Violin and Piano, op. 47, known by its dedication to a virtuoso of that name, has won particular renown. The last two cello sonatas, op. 102, in turn, are important examples of the composer's "late" style. Beethoven also wrote six piano trios (for piano, violin, and cello), five string trios (violin, viola, cello), and various other chamber works in a variety of combinations for strings, winds, and piano.

Beethoven cultivated the genre of variations throughout his life. His first published work, in fact, was a set of keyboard variations on a march tune, issued in 1782 (WoO 63). The themes he varied in these early years were sometimes of his own invention but more often taken from other composers, including several by Mozart and one by his Bonn patron Count Waldstein. Later in life he preferred to create variations on his own themes, as in the Variations for Piano, op. 35, which would later become the basis for the finale of the "Eroica" Symphony. Some of his variations are independent works, while others function as individual movements within larger works (such as the middle movement of the "Appassionata" Sonata for Piano, op. 57). The monumental "Diabelli" Variations, op. 120 (1823), constitute a veritable encyclopedia of variation techniques. In 1819, Anton Diabelli, a Viennese composer and publisher, had invited a number of his contemporaries (including Schubert, Czerny, and Archduke Rudolph, as well as Beethoven) to contribute one variation for piano on a brief waltz melody of Diabelli's own invention. In his characteristic way, Beethoven turned the simple melody inside out and upside down, showing its potential in multiple ways through no fewer than thirty-three variations, the penultimate one an enormous fugue. Beethoven also wrote variations for various chamber combinations as well, including cello and piano, violin and piano, and piano trio.

Like the piano sonatas, the sixteen string quartets—for two violins, viola, and cello—span the composer's entire creative career. This was the most prestigious of all chamber music genres, in part because of the remarkable repertory of string quartets by Haydn and Mozart. Beethoven must have been particularly self-conscious about his place within this lineage when he issued his set of six string quartets op. 18 in 1801. He modeled his quartet op. 18, no. 5, in A major, on Mozart's quartet K. 464 in the same key, an unusual act of homage that is at the same time competitive, in that it openly invites comparison of the two works.[7] The next three quartets, published in 1808 as op. 59, are altogether different: larger, more difficult, and full of the "heroic" style we associate with the Beethoven of the Third and Fifth Symphonies. The three works of op. 59 as a whole are known as the "Razumofsky Quartets" by virtue of their dedicatee, the Russian ambassador to the Austrian empire, who at the time was one of Beethoven's more important patrons. All of the subsequent quartets were substantial enough to be issued individually.

The group of five "late" quartets (opp. 127, 130, 131, 132, and 135) constitute some of the most demanding music of the nineteenth century, both technically and aesthetically. Indeed, for much of the nineteenth century and for some time into the twentieth, these works were more respected than loved. Many critics regarded them as unfortunate manifestations of Beethoven's extreme sense of isolation from the external world. These works have since come to be valued as probing explorations of the human psyche and have proven an inexhaustible source of inspiration for any number of later composers, including such diverse figures as Arnold Schoenberg, Béla Bartók, Igor Stravinsky, Elliott Carter, and George Rochberg.

Beethoven wrote a great deal more vocal music than most people realize: two settings of the Mass ordinary, an oratorio (*Christ on the Mount of Olives*), an opera (*Fidelio*), several secular cantatas and miscellaneous works for soloists, chorus, and orchestra, more than a hundred songs and individual arias, some 180 folk song arrangements, and almost fifty canons for various numbers of voices. Given this vast quantity of music, it must have galled him to read his contemporaries consistently stipulate their praise for him as the greatest living composer of *instrumental* music. In fairness to those contemporaries, this was not so much a criticism of his vocal writing as a recognition of his unique genius for instrumental works. Setting a text to music, as one anonymous critic of the op. 75 songs argued in 1811, actually "inhibited" Beethoven because it deprived him of the "broad, free field of play" he needed to display his creative gifts to the fullest.[8]

Beethoven would have gladly written more operas under the right circumstances—which is to say, a commission from an opera house—and given the right libretto. He was constantly on the search for a good text and dreamed of setting Goethe's *Faust* to music. One can only imagine what a partnership of two of the greatest artists of the time might have produced. In the end, however, he completed only one, *Fidelio* (1814), which began life as *Leonore* (1805). The libretto is an adaptation of a French drama that tells the story of a woman who disguises herself as a man and secures employment in a prison in order to free her husband, Florestan, who has been unjustly incarcerated because of his political beliefs. The so-called Third *Leonore* Overture is a brilliant encapsulation of the plot for instruments alone; it was so powerful, in fact, that it effectively overwhelmed the stage action that followed, and Beethoven wisely wrote a more concise overture and published the earlier one separately. With its theme of personal liberty and freedom of thought, *Fidelio* features many moving passages, most notably the "Contemplative Quartet" of Act I, in which the four characters on stage sing their own monologues simultaneously, the kind of thing that is simply not possible in spoken drama.

Beethoven was also constantly on the lookout for poems to set as songs for voice and piano. His poets included such leading figures as Goethe, Schiller, and Herder but also many lesser-known ones as well. Subjects range from the comical, as in *Urians Reise um die Welt* ("Urian's Journey around the World") to the serious, as in *Gegenliebe* ("Reciprocal Love"), whose melody provided the basis for the conclusion of the Choral Fantasy and in many ways adumbrated the "Ode to Joy" melody of the Ninth Symphony. He created the first true song cycle with *An die ferne Geliebte*, op. 98, a series of six songs that flow seamlessly, without interruption.

In 1809 Beethoven began a decade-long engagement with the Edinburgh publisher George Thomson to make a series of arrangements for voice, violin, cello, and piano of English, Scottish, Irish, and Welsh folk songs. Thomson specified that each setting was to open with a brief instrumental introduction, and the composer obliged by developing some portion of the melody put before him. Quite aside from the good income these settings brought in, Beethoven must have enjoyed the challenge of harmonizing melodies that do not always conform to the standard system of major and minor. "There is not one that does not bear the stamp of genius, knowledge and taste," Thomson wrote to Beethoven of one set of songs. "What delightful little *conversations* between the violin and violoncello."[9] He grumbled on more than one occasion, however, that the instrumental parts, particularly for the piano, were too technically difficult for most amateurs.

The only completed liturgical works are the two settings of the Mass Ordinary, op. 86 (commissioned by Prince Nikolaus II Esterházy), and the *Missa solemnis*, op. 123, written for the installation of Archduke Rudolph as archbishop of Olmütz in 1820 but not completed until 1823. In both works, especially the latter one, Beethoven went to extraordinary lengths to inform himself of the exact diction of the Latin words and the liturgical traditions of the Mass.[10] Indeed, he declared that his "primary goal" in writing the *Missa solemnis* had been to "arouse religious feelings and make them lasting in singers and listeners alike."[11] The sketchbooks preserve a number of other attempts at sacred works for which no immediate demand is known.

And finally, the canons, the briefest of all Beethoven's works: many of them are known only through letters to friends, where they are appended as gifts or mementos. The texts are often humorous and involve some sort of word-play. The three-voice canon *Kühl, nicht lau* ("Cool, not lukewarm"), WoO 191, for example, puns on the name of its recipient, the Danish composer Friedrich Kuhlau. Canons are rather like self-made crossword puzzles: the challenge is to create a theme that can be sung or played against itself, with voices entering in succession.

Beethoven's works are preserved in written scores, but they live in performance. And although every realization of those scores is necessarily different, traditions of performance have changed markedly over time. Nineteenth-century conductors like Richard Wagner and Gustav Mahler felt free to adjust the orchestration of the symphonies to accommodate the much larger concert halls of their day, even going so far as to add a tuba to the finale of the Ninth Symphony. This practice continued well into the twentieth century.[12]

The historically informed performance-practice movement that rose to prominence in the 1970s has taken precisely the opposite approach. Groups like Roger Norrington's London Classical Players (1978–97) and John Eliot Gardiner's Orchestre Révolutionnaire et Romantique (since 1989) use period instruments that differ markedly from those of today's modern orchestras. All the instruments of Beethoven's time have been modified to varying degrees, and orchestras and concert halls were in any case much smaller, so the experience of hearing familiar works like the symphonies played by ensembles that more nearly resemble those of earlier times can be revelatory. Textures are typically far more transparent, with individual lines standing out in greater relief. Tempos also tend to be far livelier, sometimes radically so. Norrington's 1987 recording of the slow movement of the Ninth Symphony, for example, runs just over eleven minutes, whereas the legendary 1954 Bayreuth recording by Wilhelm Furtwängler clocks in at nineteen and a half minutes. Such extreme contrasts have led scholars to question whether it is in fact the same piece.

Pianos have changed as well. The modern instrument is far larger and louder; its counterparts in Beethoven's time produced a sound that was more focused, less "mushy," as its proponents would say. The mechanisms of the two instruments also differ significantly. This compels pianists to use a lighter touch on the fortepiano, as the older instrument was known. But even these earlier instruments vary widely in size, tone, and range, and in the end there is no one "correct" instrument, new or old, for Beethoven's keyboard works. Each can help us hear these works in new ways. And the artistry of the performer remains paramount, for in the end, a score is a script waiting to be brought to life.

Chapter 11

"Beethoven"

The secret compartment of Beethoven's writing desk, discovered and opened shortly after his death, amounted to nothing less than a time capsule, for it was there that he had buried the two documents that have since contributed most to his posthumous image, which might be thought of as "Beethoven": the Heiligenstadt Testament (1802) and the letter to the Immortal Beloved (1812). These were messages, in effect, from beyond the grave, and they gave the composer a human face, one beset by physical and mental pain. When the Heiligenstadt Testament was published for the first time, in October 1827, it convinced the musical public beyond all doubt that understanding Beethoven the individual was the key to understanding his music.[1] The revelation that his art alone had held him back from suicide electrified critics and gave them more than enough reason to justify hearing his life in his works. The public now knew that the composer himself had linked his suffering to his art.

Biographical interpretations of the music became the new norm almost at once. One critic, commenting on the Ninth Symphony a year after the composer's death, identified Beethoven's suffering as a source of strength. It was these trials that had enabled him to create "a complete portrait of his soul," for the Ninth was his "autobiography, written in music." The noted Berlin critic Adolph Bernhard Marx, in turn, heard in the String Quartet in F Major, op. 135, "the deepest, innermost soul of the composer in all its richness of sentiment," an outpouring of "memories and sorrows."[2]

As more and more evidence of Beethoven's life came to light, The Scowl grew ever more severe. Anton Schindler's 1840 biography reinforced it, for he had experienced it firsthand—or so he claimed—as the composer's on-and-off personal assistant in the 1820s. Schindler was the first to publish the letter to the Immortal Beloved, another relic of personal suffering. No wonder his readers accepted at face value his report of the composer's explanation of the opening of the Fifth Symphony as "fate pounding at the portal."

The idea of autobiographical music inspired the generation of composers who came of age in Beethoven's wake. They recognized that while they could not imitate his style, they could readily promote their music as a projection of their own inner selves. Hector Berlioz encouraged listeners to hear his *Symphonie fantastique: Episode in the Life of an Artist* (1830) as a portrayal of his unhappy affair with the Irish actress Harriet Smithson, and he made sure that the Parisian press knew about the work's backstory. Robert Schumann wrote himself into his music in similar ways, using a veil of easily decoded musical ciphers in his *Carnaval* (1835), for piano, to portray himself and his circle of friends. Franz Liszt depicted his travels throughout Europe by associating the names of specific places with a number of his works for piano. Richard Wagner called attention to his personal experience of a storm at sea as the inspiration for the overture to *The Flying Dutchman*.

Critics consequently began to assume that all music—or at least all instrumental music—was somehow autobiographical. They heard Chopin's Mazurkas and Polonaises as outpourings of patriotism for their creator's native Poland. Bedřich Smetana was quite explicit when he gave his String Quartet No. 1 (1876) the subtitle "From My Life" and glossed the opening of its finale as a recreation of the high-pitched ringing that signaled the onset of his deafness. By this point, however, a noted Viennese critic could complain that "a composer could actually write 'From My Life' above each of his pieces of music, because from where should he otherwise take his music, unless he steals it?"[3]

Closely related to the belief that instrumental music could be autobiographical was the expectation that music without words could engage with philosophical and even metaphysical ideas. Composers and critics alike looked to Beethoven as a model, particularly to such works as the "Eroica" Symphony (about heroism), the "Pastoral" Symphony (about nature), and the Fifth Symphony (about "fate," if Schindler's report is to be believed, and it was). Wagner, on the other hand, argued that Beethoven had recognized the expressive limits of purely instrumental music and had shown the way toward the "Music of the Future" in the Ninth Symphony by introducing voices and text in the finale.

The Ninth's finale thus became an aesthetic battleground between those who, like Wagner, considered it a blueprint for the future of the art, and those who considered it an aberration, a one-time experiment Beethoven had pursued no further. The conductor Hans von Bülow, who allied himself with the latter group, consistently performed the Ninth without its finale. The like-minded Johannes Brahms, in turn, constructed the finale of his own First Symphony (1876) around a theme that blatantly evokes the "Ode to Joy" melody precisely in order to emphasize his own work's exclusive reliance on instruments alone. No wonder, then, that von Bülow would call Brahms's First "Beethoven's Tenth."

In the meantime, "Beethoven" was becoming monumental. An enormous statue of the composer went up in 1845 in the main square of Bonn, his birthplace. Others soon followed. They all scowl. The one in Vienna by the sculptor Caspar Clemens von Zumbusch, erected in 1880, literally looks down on us. More remarkable still is the statue created by Max Klinger for the 1902 exhibit of the Secession artists in Vienna. It portrays Beethoven as an ancient

Max Klinger's statue was the centerpiece of the Beethoven exhibition mounted by Vienna's Secession art movement in 1902. This larger-than-life polychrome likeness portrays the composer as a Greek god or perhaps philosopher. The eagle normally associated with Zeus recoils in his presence. *Peter Endig/EPA/ Shutterstock, 8213635b*

Greek deity, seated on a throne, draped by a cloth; an eagle before him recoils from the projected aura of intensity.

The music itself was monumentalized in an edition of the composer's complete works published by Breitkopf & Härtel between 1862 and 1865 in some twenty-five oversized volumes. Musicians, critics, and historians now had access in a single place to almost everything Beethoven had written. Biographies followed in great number, and scholars began to decipher the hieroglyphic sketchbooks in an attempt to understand the utterances of a figure they regarded increasingly as a musical Sphinx.

The cult of Beethoven in German-speaking lands was more than just musical. It carried significant political and nationalistic overtones. His works provided the repertorial backbone of the massive music festivals that proliferated in the middle of the nineteenth century. The performers were at first largely amateurs, and for this reason the gatherings carried all the more powerful political overtones, for large public assemblies were otherwise severely restricted at the time. Wolfgang Robert Griepenkerl's 1838 novella *Das Musikfest, oder: Die Beethovener* (*The Music Festival, or: The Beethovenians*) takes place against the backdrop of one such festival whose centerpiece is the Ninth Symphony. Musical-political conservatives plot against its performance and succeed in repressing this "revolutionary" music with its message of brotherhood and social equality.

The centenary of the composer's birth, in 1870, fell in the middle of the Franco-Prussian War, when German nationalism was approaching new heights, and Beethoven—or rather, "Beethoven"— provided the ideal cultural icon. Wagner's widely read essay marking the event centers on the composer's Germanness at a time when the nation-state of Germany, long an ideal, was on the cusp of becoming a reality.[4] Such aggressive claims of culture would only intensify in the decades that followed, culminating in the appropriation of Beethoven's art by the Nazi regime in 1933–45. The Third Reich used his works widely in its political rituals and propaganda films.

Klaus Kammerichs' *Beethon*, a concrete statue erected in 1986 outside the Beethoven-Halle in Bonn, plays on the composer's name: "Beton" is German for "concrete." When viewed directly, it appears straightforward enough, but from an angle it reveals itself as a series of recessed flattened shapes. The monument, in keeping with more recent attitudes toward the composer, is playful and something less than monumental. *Shutterstock (83074585 and 440488582)*

Paradoxically, the Allies co-opted his music to rally hearts and minds to their own cause. The opening rhythm of the Fifth Symphony (short-short-short-LONG), Morse code for the letter "V," became the sonic icon of "V for Victory."

From the extreme right to the extreme left, political ideologies of every stripe have laid claim to Beethoven. Communist regimes of the Cold War era pointed to his message of egalitarianism. During the 1970 bicentennial celebrations, Willi Stoph, the de facto head of the East German state, declared that Beethoven's music "culminates in the future image of a creative society, freed from exploitation and repression." The ideas that he "shaped musically in his compositions" would ultimately be realized in the "victorious struggle of the working class" in a socialist society. The West, Stoph maintained, had sought to remove the connection between Beethoven and the *Volk*, exploiting his music for purely commercial gain and ignoring the social implications of his creations.[5] Celebrations in the West, by contrast, emphasized the universality of Beethoven's music. In 1972, the Council of Europe adopted the melody of the Ninth Symphony's "Ode to Joy" as its wordless anthem, and it serves that same function today for that organization's successor, the European Union.

The Ninth has become an icon of freedom in recent decades. Chilean women sang the Ode to Joy melody (as *El Himno de la Alegria*) outside the prisons where their husbands, brothers, fathers, and sons were incarcerated during the era of Augusto Pinochet's repressive regime of the 1970s and 1980s. Leonard Bernstein conducted the Ninth in Berlin shortly after the fall of the Wall in late 1989, substituting *Freiheit* ("Freedom") for *Freude* ("Joy") in the finale. The idea goes back to an urban legend of sorts that began to circulate after Beethoven's time, that Schiller's "joy" was in fact a code word for "freedom."[6]

That same year, students protesting in Beijing's Tiananmen Square played the "Ode to Joy" over loudspeakers to drown out government broadcasts.[7] Six years later, the same government that had been under assault by those protestors hosted the United Nations' Fourth World Conference on Women, and the event's opening ceremony included a 126-piece all-female orchestra and workers' chorus performing the Ninth.[8] In Japan, group participation is paramount. Performances by choruses of thousands are regular occurrences, especially around New Year's. Audience members often join in the singing as well, creating what one journalist has dubbed "transcendental karaoke."[9]

Not all responses to the Ninth have been so positive. Some find its optimism oppressive. "Those who choose Elysium," as Beethoven biographer Maynard Solomon observed, "yield up their individuality to the group," and the massed choral portions of Beethoven's setting reinforce this impression, for "fraternity is intolerant of difference."[10] In Anthony Burgess's *A Clockwork Orange* and Stanley Kubrick's movie version of the novel, the Ninth becomes an instrument of violence, torture, and repression.

Pushback against "Beethoven" has been strongest around the time of anniversaries. The decade of the 1920s (with its double commemorations of 1920 and 1927) witnessed a turn toward expressive objectivity in all the arts, including music, which led Hermann Abert, one of the leading music historians of his generation, to observe that "an exasperated attitude toward Beethoven is now making itself felt among younger persons. They find his pathos oppressive, exaggerated, even intolerable; they consider his pointed subjectivity a downright calamity for the art."[11] The bicentennial celebrations in 1970 elicited even sharper critical responses. The "metacollage" *Ludwig van* by the Argentinian composer Mauricio Kagel proved especially controversial. The score consists of fragments literally cut and pasted from Beethoven's published works; any number of musicians can realize Kagel's piece by playing any portions of it they wish on an instrument of their choice, in any order and in any combination. The effect is to defamiliarize the music: we hear snippets of works we know in entirely new contexts, timbres, and combinations. Intentional (but unprescribed) distortions of volume, tempo, and timbre enhance the sense of alienation. "The music of the past," as Kagel noted, "should also be performed as music of the present."[12] His surreal black-and-white film of the same name, also from 1970, is an overt critique of the contemporary culture industry and its objectification of Beethoven and his music. Scowling busts play a prominent role.

The challenge of making Beethoven sound fresh lies at the heart of the Norwegian sound artist Leif Inge's *9 Beet Stretch*, which elongates a single recording of the Ninth Symphony over a span of twenty-four hours without any distortion of pitch. The first movement runs about five and half hours, the finale eight and a half.[13] For those who have the time, it is indeed revelatory. Anyone who has heard the open fifths at the very beginning in slow motion will likely hear any subsequent "normal" performance quite differently.

Performers continue to wrestle with Beethoven, at times almost literally. At the Ojai (California) Festival in June 2018, the violinist Patricia Kopatchinskaja presented a program entitled "Bye Bye Beethoven," which ended with a deconstruction of the Violin Concerto. The orchestra musicians began to leave the stage shortly before the end of the finale, knocking over their stands in the process, as if in protest, and the soloist, who had soldiered bravely on alone, crumpled to the floor before finishing, drowned out by a grotesquely amplified and intentionally distorted Beethovenian mashup.[14] The music had collapsed, in effect, under the weight of its own tradition.

In the meantime, Beethoven's hold on popular culture continues unabated. Of memorabilia there is no end. The collection of the Biblioteca Beethoveniana in Muggia (Trieste), Italy, houses more than 11,000 items that range from sculptures and paintings to advertisements, postage stamps, medals, coins, pins, lamps, neckties, wine bottles, pipes, and matchboxes.[15]

Filmmakers recognized Beethoven's potential early on. The composer's love life was the focus of the Austrian silent film *Der Märtyrer seines Herzens* ("The Martyr of His Heart," 1918), and in 1920, Bell & Howell produced a short silent film entitled *Beethoven's Moonlight Sonata*, in which the composer overhears a young woman playing his music on the piano and offers to play for her himself. "Snuff the candles and I will improvise for her in the moonlight," he declares. With the house lights turned down, the theater organist would no doubt have supplied the necessary music to extend well beyond the film's three minutes. More extended biopics soon followed, most notably *Un grand amour de Beethoven* ("A Great Love of Beethoven," 1937), directed by Abel Gance, again focusing on the composer's love life, as does *Immortal Beloved* (1994). One prominent online database lists more than a thousand films, documentaries, or television productions that use the composer's music in their soundtracks. Beethoven can be a presence even when we don't hear him: a camera sweep of Norman Bates's bedroom in Alfred Hitchcock's *Psycho* (1960) reveals that this decidedly unheroic character has been listening to a recording of the "Eroica."

Songwriters, in turn, have mined Beethoven's catalog repeatedly. Walter Murphy reworked the opening of the Fifth Symphony into his "Fifth of Beethoven" (1976), which figured prominently a year later in the soundtrack to the film *Saturday Night Fever*. In "Questions" (1976), Manfred Mann added words to a rather less well known but no less arresting source: the slow movement of the Violin Sonata in C minor, op. 30, no. 2. Billy Joel underlaid a text to the slow movement of "Pathétique" Sonata (op. 13) to create the song "This Night" (1984). The rapper Nas sampled the Bagatelle in A minor, WoO 59 ("Für Elise") in his "I Can" (2003), and Alicia Keys drew on the opening movement of the "Moonlight" Sonata (op. 27, no. 2) for her "Piano & I" (2011).

What might Beethoven have thought of all this? He in fact sanctioned a reworking of the slow movement of his Piano Sonata op. 2, no. 1, in 1807 as a song, with a text by his lifelong friend Wegeler ("My happiness has disappeared! My peace is gone!"). As to performances that seek to transform his music more radically, let us not forget Czerny's account of Beethoven moving his listeners to tears through his keyboard improvisation and then mocking those tears as soon as he stopped playing. Beethoven could reflect on his own art from multiple perspectives.

Listeners across the globe have done so as well. The appeal of Beethoven's music transcends differences in race, nationality, creed, age, and sex. "That dubious cliché about music being the universal language," as Leonard Bernstein observed in 1970, "almost comes true with Beethoven. No composer who has ever lived speaks so directly to so many people."[16] His music is profound yet approachable: it draws us in even while challenging us. We hear in it something that captures the human condition in ways that words and visual images cannot. Our responses are for that very reason all the more visceral and profound.

Beethoven had every reason to portray himself as a modern-day Orpheus, that mythic musician whose art was so magical that it allowed him to move back and forth between the worlds of the living and the dead. Beethoven's music helps us understand—and even believe—the core element of that myth: the power of music.

CHRONOLOGY

1770   Born in Bonn, probably on December 16; baptized
on December 17

1778   Appears in public as a pianist for the first time

1782   Begins musical studies with Christian Gottlob Neefe and
serves as court organist in his absence. First published
work appears, a set of keyboard variations.

1784   Appointed court organist in Bonn

1787   Travels to Vienna to pursue musical studies but is called
back to Bonn because of the illness of his mother, who
dies in July

1792   Travels again to Vienna, arriving in early November,
never to return to Bonn. His teachers over the next
few years include Joseph Haydn, Johann Georg
Albrechtsberger, and Antonio Salieri. He appears
frequently in aristocratic salons as a pianist and wins
special renown for his abilities as an improviser.

1795   Op. 1 Piano Trios published in Vienna

1796   Journeys to Prague, Nuremberg, Berlin

1800   Premiere of the First Symphony

1801   Acknowledges to a few close friends the onset of
deafness

1802   Confesses in a lengthy document now known as the
            Heiligenstadt Testament that his growing deafness has
            driven him to the brink of suicide; the document is not
            discovered until after his death

1803   Premiere of the Second Symphony, the Third Piano
            Concerto, and the oratorio *Christ on the Mount of Olives*,
            all in a performance organized by the composer

1804   Premiere of the "Eroica" Symphony in a private
            performance in the Viennese palace of Prince Lobkowitz

1805   First performance of the opera *Leonore*, later to be
            reworked (in 1814) as *Fidelio*

1807   Premiere of the Fourth Symphony

1808   Publication of the String Quartets op. 59. Premiere
            of the Fifth and Sixth Symphonies, the Fourth Piano
            Concerto, and the Choral Fantasy in a single all-
            Beethoven concert in Vienna

1809   Offered the position of music director at the court of
            Jérôme Bonaparte, King of Westphalia, but is persuaded
            to remain in Vienna on the promise of an annuity funded
            by three noble patrons

1810   Proposes marriage to Therese Malfatti but is rejected.
            Begins writing folk song arrangements for the Scottish
            publisher George Thomson.

1812   Passionate love affair with the unidentified woman now
            known as the "Immortal Beloved." His deafness, after a
            period of relative stability, becomes even more severe,
            and he withdraws into an ever-smaller circle of friends
            and assistants.

1813   Premiere of the Seventh Symphony

1814   Active in the musical events surrounding the Congress
            of Vienna, which opens on 1 November and continues
            until June 1815. Premiere of the Eighth Symphony.

1816   Assumes guardianship of his nephew, Karl, and begins a
            lengthy legal battle with his sister-in-law, Karl's mother.

Composes the Piano Sonata op. 101, widely regarded as the first work of his "late" style.

1819   Publishes the "Hammerklavier" Sonata, op. 106

1821   Completes the three last piano sonatas, opp. 109, 110, 111

1824   Premiere of the Ninth Symphony

1825   Completes the String Quartet op. 127, the first of the five "late" quartets

1827   Dies in Vienna on March 26. Buried in the district of Währing on March 29. His remains are transferred to Vienna's Central Cemetery in 1888.

NOTES

Introduction

1. The report by Anselm Hüttenbrenner, written in 1860, is excerpted in *Thayer's Life of Beethoven* (hereafter Thayer-Forbes), rev. and ed. Elliot Forbes (Princeton: Princeton University Press, 1967), 1050–51.

Chapter 1

1. Anonymous, "Nachrichten: Wien," *Allgemeine musikalische Zeitung* 18 (February 21, 1816): 121.

2. Goethe, *Dichtung und Wahrheit* (1811–1814), in his *Werke: Hamburger Ausgabe*, 14 vols., ed. Erich Trunz et al. (Munich: Beck, 1981), 9:283.

3. Chrétien Urhan, "Feuilleton, Revue musicale. Musique. Premier concert du Conservatoire.—Symphonie avec choeur de Beethoven," *Le Temps*, January 25, 1838, as quoted in David B. Levy, "Early Performances of Beethoven's Ninth Symphony: A Study of Five Cities" (PhD diss., University of Rochester, Eastman School of Music, 1980), 323; Alexandre Oulibicheff, *Beethoven: Ses critiques et ses glossateurs* (Paris: Jules Gavelot, 1857), 262.

4. Julian Schmidt, *Geschichte der deutschen Nationalliteratur im neunzehnten Jahrhundert*, 2 vols. (Leipzig: Herbig, 1853), 2:410. Unless otherwise indicated, all translations are my own.

5. Anonymous, "Recension: Musée musical des Clavicinistes," *Allgemeine musikalische Zeitung mit besonderer Rücksicht auf den österreichischen Kaiserstaat* 1 (February 27, 1817): 66.

6. Friedrich Schlegel, "Lyceums-Fragment 55" (1797), in *Kritische Friedrich-Schlegel-Ausgabe*, ed. Ernst Behler et al. (Munich: F. Schöningh, 1958–), 2:154.

7. E. T. A. Hoffmann, "Recension: *Sinfonie... par Louis van Beethoven... Oeuvre 67*," *Allgemeine musikalische Zeitung* 12 (July 4, 1810): 633–34.

8. Letter of ca. 1798, *Briefwechsel: Gesamtausgabe* (hereafter *BGA*), ed. Sieghard Brandenburg, 7 vols. (Munich: G. Henle, 1996–1998), no. 35 (1:43); Beethoven, *The Letters of Beethoven* (hereafter Anderson), ed. Emily Anderson, 3 vols. (London: Macmillan, 1961), no. 30 (1:32).

9. See Mark Evan Bonds, "Irony and Incomprehensibility: Beethoven's 'Serioso' String Quartet in F minor, Op. 95, and the Path to the Late Style," *Journal of the American Musicological Society* 70 (2017): 285–356.

10. Carl Czerny, "Further Recollections of Beethoven," *Cock's Musical Miscellany* 1, no. 6 (August 2, 1852): 65–66, quoted in *Beethoven aus der Sicht seiner Zeitgenossen* (hereafter Kopitz-Cadenbach), ed. Klaus Martin Kopitz and Rainer Cadenbach, 2 vols. (Munich: G. Henle, 2009), 1:215.

11. A. G., "Conservatoire Impérial de Musique, Ier. et IIme. exercices des élèves," *Les Tablettes de Polymnie* 2 (March 20, 1811): 310–11.

12. Jeremy Denk, "Congratulate Yourself, Beethoven," http://jeremydenk.net/blog/2011/07/10/congratulate-yourself-beethoven-3/.

13. Gustav Nottebohm, *Zweite Beethoveniana* (Leipzig: C. F. Peters, 1887), 182n.

14. Letter of early November 1804, *BGA* no. 197 (1:227); Anderson no. 98 (1:118–19).

15. Letter to Wegeler, June 29, 1801, *BGA* no. 65 (1:81); Anderson no. 51 (1:62); Karl Bursy, quoted in Kopitz-Cadenbach, 1:173. On the coincidence of the Fifth and Sixth Symphonies and their similarities in spite of their outward differences, see Raymond Knapp, "A Tale of Two Symphonies: Converging Narratives of Divine Reconciliation in Beethoven's Fifth and Sixth," *Journal of the American Musicological Society* 53 (2000): 291–343.

16. Beethoven to Breitkopf & Härtel, February 28, 1812, *BGA* no. 555 (2:245–46); Anderson no. 351 (1:359).

Chapter 2

1. Barry Cooper, *Beethoven and the Creative Process* (Oxford: Clarendon Press, 1990), 5, 1.

2. See Maynard Solomon, "Beethoven's Birth Year," in his *Beethoven Essays* (Cambridge, MA: Harvard University Press, 1988), 35–42.

3. Christian Gottlob Neefe, "Nachricht von der churfürstlich-cöllnischen Hofcapelle zu Bonn und andern Tonkünstlern daselbst," *Magazin der Musik* 1 (1783): 395.

4. Letter to Breitkopf & Härtel, November 22, 1809, *BGA* no. 408 (2:88); Anderson no. 228 (1:246).

5. Julia Ronge, "Beethoven liest musiktheoretische Fachliteratur," in *Beethoven liest*, ed. Bernhard R. Appel and Julia Ronge (Bonn: Beethoven-Haus, 2016), 27.

6. Letter of January 23, 1782, to Leopold Mozart, in Wolfgang Amadeus Mozart, *Briefe und Aufzeichnungen: Gesamtausgabe*, expanded ed., 8 vols., ed. Wilhelm A. Bauer, Otto Erich Deutsch, and Ulrich Konrad (Kassel: Bärenreiter, 2005), 3:193.

7. Anton Schindler, *Biographie von Ludwig van Beethoven*, 3rd ed., 2 vols. (Münster: Aschendorff, 1860), 1:18.

8. Thayer-Forbes, 89. See also Dieter Haberl, "Beethovens erste Reise nach Wien: Die Datierung seiner Schulreise zu W. A. Mozart," *Neues Musikwissenschaftliches Jahrbuch* 14 (2006): 215–55.

9. Ignaz von Seyfried, *Ludwig van Beethoven's Studien im Generalbasse, Contrapuncte, und in der Compositions-Lehre* (Vienna: Haslinger, 1832), 6–7. Translation from Thayer-Forbes, 206–7. For an account of this "duel," see Tia DeNora, *Beethoven and the Construction of Genius: Musical Politics in Vienna, 1792–1803* (Berkeley: University of California Press, 1995), 147–69.

10. On Beethoven's early Viennese patrons and system of musical patronage in Vienna, see DeNora, *Beethoven and the Construction of Genius*, especially 74–77.

11. Alice M. Hanson, "Incomes and Outgoings in the Vienna of Beethoven and Schubert," *Music & Letters* 64 (1985): 178.

12. Franz Wegeler and Ferdinand Ries, *Biographische Notizen über Ludwig van Beethoven* (Koblenz: K. Bädeker, 1838), 33.

13. Wegeler and Ries, *Biographische Notizen*, 119–20.

14. Letter of November 2, 1793, *BGA* no. 11 (1:17); Anderson no. 7 (1:11).

15. John Russell, *A Tour in Germany*, 2nd ed., 2 vols. (Edinburgh: Archibald Constable, 1825), 2:273–74.

16. The report by Louis Baron de Trémont is quoted in Kopitz-Cadenbach, 2:1004.

17. Letter to B. Schott's Söhne, September 17, 1824, *BGA* no. 1881 (5:368); Anderson no. 1308 (3:1141).

Chapter 3

1. On *Bildung*, see Walter Horace Bruford, *The German Tradition of Self-Cultivation: Bildung from Humboldt to Thomas Mann* (Cambridge: Cambridge University Press, 1975); Rebekka Horlacher, *The Educated Subject and the German Concept of Bildung: A Comparative Cultural History* (New York: Routledge, 2016). On the word as a neologism, see Steven Lukes, *Individualism* (New York: Harper & Row, 1973), 1.

2. Letter to Breitkopf & Härtel, November 22, 1809, *BGA* no. 408 (2:88); Anderson no. 228 (1:246).

3. Louis Baron de Trémont, quoted in Kopitz-Cadenbach, 2:1005.

4. Ludwig van Beethoven, *Beethovens Tagebuch: 1812-1818*, 2nd ed., ed. Maynard Solomon (Bonn: Beethoven-Haus, 2005), 29-30. Translation from Maynard Solomon, "Beethoven's *Tagebuch*," in his *Beethoven Essays*, 246. In addition to a complete translation, Solomon's essay includes a concise history of the text, which was transmitted through various copies of Beethoven's original, now lost.

5. Beethoven, *Beethovens Tagebuch*, 30; translations from Solomon, "Beethoven's *Tagebuch*," 247.

6. Letter to Hans Georg Nägeli, September 9, 1824, *BGA* no. 1873 (5:362); Anderson no. 1306 (3:1139).

7. Beethoven, *Beethovens Tagebuch*, 41, 45; translations from Solomon, "Beethoven's *Tagebuch*," 254, 258.

8. Beethoven, *Beethovens Tagebuch*, 72, 104; translations amended from Solomon, "Beethoven's *Tagebuch*," 274, 294.

9. Letter to "Emilie M. in Hamburg," *BGA* no. 585 (2:274); Anderson no. 376 (1:381). On the presumed authenticity of this letter, see Lewis Lockwood, *Beethoven: The Music and the Life* (New York: Norton, 2005), 8-12.

10. Letter of September 17, 1824, to B. Schott's Söhne, Mainz, *BGA* no. 1881 (5:368); Anderson no. 1308 (3:1141).

11. Ludwig Tieck, "Symphonien" (1799), in Wilhelm Heinrich Wackenroder, *Sämtliche Werke und Briefe*, ed. Silvio Vietta and Richard Littlejohns, 2 vols. (Heidelberg: Carl Winter Universitätsverlag, 1991), 1:241. Hoffmann, "Recension: *Sinfonie ... par Louis van Beethoven ... Oeuvre 67*," 633.

12. On Beethoven as a Catholic, see Nicholas J. Chong, "Beethoven's Catholicism: A Reconsideration" (PhD diss., Columbia University, 2016). See also Maynard Solomon, "The Quest for Faith" in his *Beethoven Essays*, 216–29.

13. Beethoven, *Beethovens Tagebuch*, 66. On Beethoven's connections to Freemasonry, see Maynard Solomon, *Late Beethoven: Music, Thought, Imagination* (Berkeley: University of California Press, 2003), 135–78.

14. Beethoven, *Beethovens Tagebuch*, 57–64; translations from Solomon, "Beethoven's *Tagebuch*," 265–69. See also Solomon, *Late Beethoven*, 164–68.

15. Annotation to Herder's poem "Macht des Gesanges," transcribed in Ludwig Nohl, *Beethovens Brevier* (Leipzig: Ernst Julius Günther, 1870), 104; see also Solomon, *Late Beethoven*, 43.

16. Letter to Therese Malfatti, late May 1810, *BGA* no. 442 (2:122); Anderson no. 258 (1:273).

17. Beethoven, *Beethovens Tagebuch*, 48; translation from Solomon, "Beethovens Tagebuch," 259. Solomon points out that the scansion marks suggest that Beethoven considered setting this text to music.

18. *BGA* no. 106 (1:122); Anderson Appendix A (3:1352).

19. Letter to Wegeler, November 6, 1801, *BGA* no. 70 (1:89); Anderson no. 54 (1:68).

Chapter 4

1. By far the best treatment of Beethoven's deafness is Robin Wallace, *Hearing Beethoven: A Story of Musical Loss and Discovery* (Chicago: University of Chicago Press, 2018). My account draws heavily on Wallace's sensitive and insightful research.

2. Letter to Wegeler, June 29, 1801, *BGA* no. 65 (1:80); Anderson no. 51 (1:60).

3. *BGA* no. 106 (1:121–25). For a translation of the complete text, see Maynard Solomon, *Beethoven*, 2nd ed. (New York: Schirmer Books, 1998), 151–54.

4. *BGA* no. 106 (1:123).

5. Wallace, *Hearing Beethoven*, 31, 26.

6. Wallace, *Hearing Beethoven*, 134.

7. Wallace, *Hearing Beethoven*, 139–49.

8. *Der Korrespondent von und für Deutschland* (Nuremberg) 9, no. 340 (6 December 1814): 1417–18, quoted in Klaus Martin Kopitz, "Beethoven

und die Zarenfamilie: Bekanntes und Unbekanntes zur Akademie vom 29. November 1814 sowie zur Polonaise op. 89," *Bonner Beethoven-Studien* 5 (2006): 143. Ignaz Ritter von Seyfried made similar comments in 1832; see Thayer-Forbes, 371.

9. Thayer-Forbes, 810–11.

10. For an account of the first performance of the Ninth, see Thomas Forrest Kelly, *First Night: Five Musical Premieres* (New Haven: Yale University Press, 2000), 108–79.

11. Letter to Joseph Wilhelm von Schaden, September 15, 1787, *BGA* no. 3 (1:5); Anderson no. 1 (1:4).

12. See Elaine Sisman, "Music and the Labyrinth of Melancholy: Traditions and Paradoxes in C. P. E. Bach and Beethoven," in *The Oxford Handbook of Music and Disability Studies,* ed. Blake Howe, Stephanie Jensen-Moulton, Neil Lerner, and Joseph Straus (New York: Oxford University Press, 2016), 590–617.

13. Owen Jander, " 'Let Your Deafness No Longer Be a Secret—Even in Art': Self-Portraiture and the Third Movement of the C-Minor Symphony," *Beethoven Forum* 8 (2000): 25–70.

14. Letter to Wegeler, November 6, 1801, *BGA* no. 70 (1:89); Anderson no. 54 (1:68).

Chapter 5

1. Wegeler and Ries, *Biographische Notizen,* 117.

2. For a concise history of the riddle surrounding the identity of the Immortal Beloved and an argument in favor of Antonie Brentano, see Solomon, *Beethoven,* 207–46. For a rebuttal and an argument in favor of Josephine von Brunsvik-Deym-Stackelberg, see Rita Steblin, "New Evidence for Josephine as the 'Immortal Beloved' Involving Beethoven and England," *Musical Times* 160, no. 1947 (2019): 15–41.

3. *BGA* no. 582 (2:271); Anderson no. 373 (1:376).

4. Beethoven, *Beethovens Tagebuch,* 29–30; translation from Solomon, "Beethoven's *Tagebuch,*" 246.

5. See Steblin, "New Evidence," 19.

6. Anton Schindler, *Biographie von Ludwig van Beethoven* (Münster: Aschendorff, 1840), 29.

7. Schindler, *Biographie von Ludwig van Beethoven*, 34.

8. On the reception of the work, see Lawrence Kramer, "Hands On, Lights Off: The 'Moonlight' Sonata and the Birth of Sex at the Piano," in his *Musical Meaning: Toward a Critical History* (Berkeley: University of California Press, 2002), 29–50.

9. Letter of May 8, 1816, *BGA* no. 933 (3:257); Anderson no. 632 (2:577). The key word is "Frauenfeind," literally, "an enemy of women."

10. Birgit Lodes, "Zur musikalischen Passgenauigkeit von Beethovens Kompositionen mit Widmungen an Adelige: *An die ferne Geliebte* op. 98 in neuer Deutung," in *Widmungen bei Haydn und Beethoven: Personen, Strategien, Praktiken*, ed. Bernhard R. Appel and Armin Raab (Bonn: Verlag Beethoven-Haus, 2015), 171–202.

Chapter 6

1. Georg August Griesinger, *Biographische Notizen über Joseph Haydn* (Leipzig: Breitkopf & Härtel, 1810), 24.

2. Letter to Hoffmeister & Kühnel, ca. September 20, 1803, *BGA* no. 157 (1:183); Anderson no. 82 (1:97–98).

3. Letter to Franz Anton Hoffmeister, January 15, 1801, *BGA* no. 54 (1:64); Anderson no. 44 (1:48). See also Maynard Solomon, "Beethoven's *Magazin der Kunst*," in his Solomon, *Beethoven Essays*, 193–204.

4. Beethoven, *Beethovens Tagebuch*, 45; translation amended from Solomon, "Beethoven's *Tagebuch*," 258. The report by Louis Baron de Trémont concerning Napoleon is quoted in Kopitz-Cadenbach, 2:1008.

5. Letter of April 5, 1809, *BGA* no. 375 (2:58); Anderson no. 209 (1:224–25).

6. Johann Friedrich Reichardt, *Vertraute Briefe, geschrieben auf einer Reise nach Wien und den österreichischen Staaten zu Ende des Jahres 1808 und zu Anfang 1809* (Amsterdam: Kunst- und Industrie-Comptoir, 1810), 2 vols., 1:254–55.

7. Letter of sometime after May 19, 1818, *BGA* no. 1259 (4:190–91); Anderson no. 903 (2:766–67).

8. Letter to C. F. Peters, February 20, 1823, *BGA* no. 1575 (5:52); Anderson no. 1158 (3:1020).

9. Letter to Andreas Streicher, July–September 1796, *BGA* no. 22 (1:32); Anderson no. 18 (1:25).

10. Albert Christoph Dies, *Biographische Nachrichten von Joseph Haydn* (Vienna: Camesina, 1810), 75.

11. Letter of December 28, 1782, to his father, in Mozart, *Briefe und Aufzeichnungen*, 3:245. The concertos in question are K. 413, 414, and 415.

12. Anonymous, "*X Variationen pour le clavecin . . . par L. van Beethoven*," *Allgemeine musikalische Zeitung* 1 (June 19, 1799): 607. The work under review is *Ten Variations on the Duettino "La stessa, la stessima,"* WoO 73; the theme is from Antonio Salieri's opera *Falstaff*.

13. Anonymous, "*Tre sonate . . . dal S. Luigi van Beethoven. Op. 12*," *Allgemeine musikalische Zeitung* 1 (June 5, 1799): 571.

14. See Mark Evan Bonds, *The Beethoven Syndrome: Hearing Music as Autobiography* (New York: Oxford University Press, 2020).

15. Letter to Breitkopf & Härtel, April 22, 1801, *BGA* 59 (1:69); Anderson no. 48 (1:53).

16. Anonymous, "Wien: Musikalisches Tagebuch vom Monat März," *Allgemeine musikalische Zeitung* 28 (May 10, 1826): 310–11.

Chapter 7

1. The comment ("Östreich löhne Napoleon") appears at the beginning of the second movement. See Ludwig van Beethoven, *Werke*, III:3, *Klavierkonzerte II*, ed. Hans-Werner Küthen (Munich: G. Henle, 1996), xiii.

2. Kopitz, "Beethoven und die Zarenfamilie": 146. On the value of the gift, see Alice M. Hanson, *Musical Life in Biedermeier Vienna* (Cambridge: Cambridge University Press, 1985), 21. On the appropriateness of the polonaise for the Russian empress, see Birgit Lodes. "'Le congrès danse': Set Form and Improvisation in Beethoven's Polonaise for Piano, Op. 89," *Musical Quarterly* 93 (2010): 414–49.

3. Letter to Beethoven from the City Magistrate of Vienna, November 16, 1815, *BGA* no. 853 (3:179). On the performances of *Fidelio*, see Maria Rößner-Richarz, "Beethoven und der Wiener Kongress aus der Perspektive von Beethovens Briefen und Dokumenten," in *Beethoven und der Wiener Kongress*, ed. Bernhard R. Appel, Joanna Cobb Biermann, William Kinderman, and Julia Ronge (Bonn: Verlag Beethoven-Haus, 2016), 116.

4. Letter of Autumn 1814, *BGA* no. 747 (3:64); Anderson no. 502 (1:474).

5. Letter written soon after June 25, 1823, *BGA* no. 1680 (5:157); Anderson no. 1194 (3:1049).

6. Letter of August 2, 1794, *BGA* no. 17 (1:26); Anderson no. 12 (1:18).

7. Letter to Johann Baptist Bach, October 27, 1819, *BGA* no. 1348 (4:331); Anderson no. 979 (2:852). See Maynard Solomon, "The Nobility Pretense," in his *Beethoven Essays*, 43–55.

8. See DeNora, *Beethoven and the Construction of Genius*, especially 37–82.

9. Ludwig Tieck, quoted in Kopitz-Cadenbach, 2:986.

10. Letter to Breitkopf & Härtel, July 26, 1809, *BGA* no. 392 (2:71); Anderson no. 220 (1:233–34).

11. See L. Poundie Burstein, "'Lebe wohl tönt überall' and a 'Reunion after So Much Sorrow': Beethoven's Op. 81a and the Journeys of 1809," *Musical Quarterly* 93 (2010): 366–413.

12. As transcribed by Julia Ronge, "Beethoven liest musiktheoretische Fachliteratur," 28.

13. Letter of March 5, 1818, *BGA* no. 1247 (4:178); Anderson no. 895 (2:760).

14. See Hanson, *Musical Life in Biedermeier Vienna*, chapter 2, "Musicians and the Austrian Police."

15. Joseph Sonnleithner to Philipp von Stahl, October 3, 1805, *BGA* no. 238 (1:267–68).

16. On the complicated history of the censorship of the libretto to *Fidelio*, see Robin Wallace, "The Curious Incident of *Fidelio* and the Censors," in *The Oxford Handbook of Music Censorship*, ed. Patricia Hall (New York: Oxford, 2015), 221–34.

17. Beethoven, *Konversationshefte*, ed. Karl-Heinz Köhler and Dagmar Beck, 11 vols. (Leipzig: Deutscher Verlag für Musik, 1972–2001), 9:168.

18. Beethoven, *Konversationshefte*, 2:279.

19. Beethoven, *Konversationshefte*, 3:288.

20. See Mark Evan Bonds, *Music as Thought: Listening to the Symphony in the Age of Beethoven* (Princeton: Princeton University Press, 2006), 92–103.

Chapter 8

1. Robert Winter, "The Sketches for the 'Ode to Joy,'" in *Beethoven, Performers, and Critics: The International Beethoven Congress Detroit 1977*, ed. Robert Winter and Bruce Carr (Detroit: Wayne State University Press, 1980), 184–90.

2. On the symphonic false starts, see Barry Cooper, "The Compositional Act: Sketches and Autographs," in *The Cambridge Companion to Beethoven*, ed. Glenn Stanley (Cambridge: Cambridge University Press, 2000), 37.

3. Douglas Johnson, "Beethoven Scholars and Beethoven's Sketches," *19th-Century Music* 2 (1978): 6.

4. Anonymous, "Nachrichten," *Allgemeine musikalische Zeitung* 7 (February 13, 1805): 321.

5. In Ludwig van Beethoven, *Werke*, I/3: *Symphonien III*, ed. Jens Dufner (Munich: G. Henle, 2013).

Chapter 9

1. The summary here follows the chronology and motivations proposed by Maynard Solomon, "The Creative Periods of Beethoven," in *Beethoven Essays*, 116–25.

2. Quoted in Karl-Heinz Köhler, "The Conversation Books: Aspects of a New Picture of Beethoven," in *Beethoven, Performers, and Critics*, 154.

3. *Wiener Journal für Theater, Musik und Mode* 1 (1806), quoted in *Ludwig van Beethoven: Die Werke im Spiegel seiner Zeit*, ed. Stefan Kunze (Laaber: Laaber-Verlag, 1987), 13. Anonymous, "Tre Sonate . . . dal S. Luigi van Beethoven," *Allgemeine musikalische Zeitung* 1 (June 5, 1799): 571.

4. Scott Burnham, *Beethoven Hero* (Princeton: Princeton University Press, 1995).

5. Holz's recollections as reported by Wilhelm von Lenz, *Beethoven: Eine Kunststudie*, 5 vols. (Kassel: Ernst Balde; Hamburg: Hoffmann & Campe, 1855–1860), 5:217.

Chapter 10

1. Letter to Breitkopf & Härtel, ca. December 18, 1802, *BGA* no. 123 (1:145); Anderson no. 67 (1:84).

2. Anonymous, "Soll man bey der Instrumentalmusik Etwas denken," *Allgemeine musikalische Zeitung* 29 (1827): 529–38, 546–54.

3. The comment appears in the first edition of the orchestral parts, issued by Breitkopf & Härtel of Leipzig in May 1809.

4. Steven M. Whiting, "Beethoven Translating Shakespeare: Dramatic Models for the Slow Movement of the String Quartet Op. 18, No. 1," *Journal of the American Musicological Society* 71 (2018): 795–838.

5. Owen Jander, "Beethoven's 'Orpheus in Hades': The 'Andante con moto' of the Fourth Piano Concerto," *19th-Century Music* 8 (1985): 195–212. Jander would later expand on this reading in his *Beethoven's "Orpheus" Concerto: The Fourth Piano Concerto in Its Cultural Context* (Hillsdale, NY: Pendragon Press, 2009).

6. Richard Wagner, *Das Kunstwerk der Zukunft* (Leipzig: Otto Wigand, 1850), 90.

7. See Jeremy Yudkin, "Beethoven's 'Mozart' Quartet," *Journal of the American Musicological Society* 45 (1992): 30–74.

8. Anonymous, "*Sechs Gesänge mit Begleit. des Pianoforte . . . von L. van Beethoven . . . Oeuvr. 75*," *Allgemeine musikalische Zeitung* 13 (August 28, 1811): 593. E. T. A. Hoffmann made much the same point in his review of the Fifth Symphony; see his "Recension: *Sinfonie . . . par Louis van Beethoven*," 633.

9. George Thomson to Beethoven, August 5, 1812, *BGA* no. 590 (2:281); translations from *Letters to Beethoven and Other Correspondence*, ed. and trans. Theodore Albrecht, 3 vols. (Lincoln: University of Nebraska Press, 1996), no. 163 (1:256).

10. See Warren Kirkendale, "New Roads to Old Ideas in Beethoven's 'Missa Solemnis'," *Musical Quarterly* 56 (1970): 665–701.

11. Letter to Johann Andreas Streicher, September 16, 1824, *BGA* no. 1875 (5:364); Anderson no. 1307 (3:1140).

12. See David Pickett, "A Comparative Survey of Rescorings in Beethoven's Symphonies," in *Performing Beethoven*, ed. Robin Stowell (Cambridge: Cambridge University Press, 1994), 205–27.

Chapter 11

1. Friedrich Rochlitz, "Den Freunden Beethovens," *Allgemeine musikalische Zeitung* 29 (October 17, 1827): 705–10.

2. Joseph Fröhlich, "Recensionen: Sinfonie, mit Schlusschor . . ." *Cäcilia* 8 (1828): 236. A. B. Marx, "Beurtheilungen: Quatuor pour 2 Violons, Alto, et Violoncelle par L. v. Beethoven. Oeuvr. 135 . . . " *Berliner Allgemeine musikalische Zeitung* 6 (1829): 169.

3. Ludwig Speidel, *Fremden-Blatt*, January 25, 1893, 7–8, as quoted in Elizabeth Way Sullivan, "Conversing in Public: Chamber Music in Vienna, 1890–1910" (PhD diss., University of Pittsburgh, 2001), 129. On the growing perception of music as an autobiographical art from 1830 onward, see Bonds, *The Beethoven Syndrome*.

4. Richard Wagner, *Beethoven* (Leipzig: E. W. Fritzsch, 1870); translated by Richard Allen as *Richard Wagner's Beethoven* (Woodbridge: Boydell, 2014).

5. Willi Stoph, address to the Konstituierende Sitzung des Komitees für die Beethoven-Ehrung der DDR, *Neues Deutschland*, March 28, 1970, quoted in Hans Heinrich Eggebrecht, *Zur Geschichte der Beethoven-Rezeption*, 2nd ed. (Laaber: Laaber-Verlag, 1994), 84; idem, "Festansprache . . . auf dem Festakt zur Beethoven-Ehrung der Deutschen Demokratischen Republik am 16. Dezember 1970," in *Bericht über den Internationalen Beethoven-Kongress 10.–12. Dezember 1970 in Berlin*, ed. Heinz Alfred Brockhaus and Konrad Niemann (Berlin: Verlag Neue Musik, 1971), 2–3. For an account of these celebrations in both East and West Germany, see David B. Dennis, *Beethoven in German Politics, 1870–1989* (New Haven: Yale University Press, 1996), 177–97.

6. See Gail K. Hart, "Schiller's 'An die Freude' and the Question of Freedom," *German Studies Review* 32 (2009): 479–93. On Bernstein's performance, see Alexander Rehding, " 'Ode to Freedom': Bernstein's Ninth at the Berlin Wall," *Beethoven Forum* 12 (2005): 38–49.

7. See Kerry Candaele and Greg Mitchell, *Journeys with Beethoven: Following the Ninth, and Beyond* (New York: Sinclair Books, 2013), 20–36, 46–87.

8. Steven Mufson, "Women's Forum Opens in China amid Disputes," *Washington Post*, August 31, 1995. https://www.washingtonpost.com/archive/politics/1995/08/31/womens-forum-opens-in-china-amid-disputes/41143272-3405-4806-9099-9254afc002cf/?utm_term=.7461f6371038. Idem, "Women's Conference Opens with Fanfare," *Washington Post*, September 5, 1995. https://www.washingtonpost.com/archive/politics/1995/09/05/womens-conference-opens-with-fanfare/870797c2-d77b-4405-961f-482bad594b9c/?utm_term=.963f39d8a014. My thanks to Michael Morse for pointing out this latter performance to me.

9. Steven R. Weisman, "Japan Sings Along with Beethoven," *New York Times*, December 29, 1990. https://www.nytimes.com/1990/12/29/arts/japan-sings-along-with-beethoven.html. See also Candaele and Mitchell, *Journeys with Beethoven*, 59–72.

10. Solomon, *Late Beethoven*, 225.

11. Hermann Abert, "Beethoven zum 26. März 1927," *Die Musik* 19 (1927): 386.

12. Mauricio Kagel, Preface to *Ludwig van: Hommage von Beethoven* (London: Universal Edition, 1970), ix.

13. For a discussion of *9 Beet Stretch*, see Alexander Rehding, *Beethoven's Symphony No. 9* (New York: Oxford University Press, 2018), 26–29, 71–81.

14. A video of the performance is available at https://www.youtube.com/watch?v=zVMDXhixQbI.

15. http://www.bibliotecabeethoveniana.it/.

16. *Bernstein on Beethoven: A Celebration in Vienna* (1970), directed by Humphrey Burton.

FURTHER READING

SCORES

The standard modern edition of the music is the *Werke*, ed. Joseph Schmidt-Görg et al. (Munich: Henle, 1961–). This set of carefully edited scores is still in progress and not likely to be finished for several decades yet. In the meantime, the older *Werke*, 37 vols. (Leipzig: Breitkopf & Härtel, 1862–1865, 1888), remains serviceable if far from ideal; it is accessible online through the International Music Score Library Project (IMSLP) at www.imslp.org. Many selections from this older edition have also been reprinted in reasonably priced editions.

THEMATIC CATALOGUE

The authoritative catalogue of the music is *Ludwig van Beethoven: Thematisch-bibliographisches Werkverzeichnis*, ed. Kurt Dorfmüller, Norbert Gertsch, and Julia Ronge, 2 vols. (Munich: G. Henle, 2014). The entry for each work provides detailed information on its origins, surviving sketches, first performance, and first and early editions, along with a brief musical notation of the opening of each work and its various movements, if any.

LETTERS AND DOCUMENTS

The meticulously annotated *Briefwechsel: Gesamtausgabe*, ed. Sieghard Brandenburg, 7 vols. (Munich: G. Henle, 1996–1998), includes letters both to and from the composer in their original languages. Emily Anderson's English translation, *The Letters of Beethoven*, 3 vols. (London: Macmillan,

1961), is supplemented by Theodore Albrecht's *Letters to Beethoven and Other Correspondence*, 3 vols. (Lincoln: University of Nebraska Press, 1996). Maynard Solomon's *Beethoven Essays* (Cambridge, MA: Harvard University Press, 1988) includes a translation of the complete diary. *Beethoven: A Documentary Study*, ed. H. C. Robbins Landon (New York: Macmillan, 1970), offers a good selection of key sources.

BIOGRAPHIES

Excellent accounts include Maynard Solomon's *Beethoven*, 2nd ed. (New York: Schirmer Books, 1998); Lewis Lockwood's *Beethoven: The Music and the Life* (New York: Norton, 2005); William Kinderman's *Beethoven*, 2nd ed. (New York: Oxford University Press, 2009); and Jan Swafford's *Beethoven: Anguish and Triumph* (Boston: Houghton Mifflin Harcourt, 2014). Solomon's focus is on Beethoven the individual, with emphasis on the composer's psychological makeup. Lockwood, Kinderman, and Swafford integrate accounts of the music and the life. Alexander Wheelock Thayer's *Beethoven* (1866–1879), revised by Elliot Forbes as *Thayer's Life of Beethoven* (Princeton: Princeton University Press, 1967), documents the composer's life year-by-year in detail and remains indispensable though in need of updating.

ICONOGRAPHY

Alessandra Comini, *The Changing Image of Beethoven: A Study in Mythmaking*, 2nd ed. (Santa Fe, NM: Sunstone Press, 2008), traces images of the composer from his lifetime into the early twentieth century. H. C. Robbins Landon's *Beethoven: A Documentary Study* (New York: Macmillan, 1970) provides a rich selection of texts as well as images.

HANDBOOKS AND ESSAY COLLECTIONS

The Beethoven Compendium, ed. Barry Cooper (London: Thames and Hudson, 1991), and *The Cambridge Companion to Beethoven*, ed. Glenn Stanley (Cambridge: Cambridge University Press, 2000) provide excellent overviews of both the life and works. *Beethoven and His World*, ed. Scott Burnham and Michael P. Steinberg (Princeton: Princeton University Press, 2000), offers more-specialized but important essays. Maynard Solomon's *Beethoven Essays* (Cambridge, MA: Harvard University Press, 1988) and *Late Beethoven: Music, Thought, Imagination* (Berkeley: University of California Press, 2003) supplement his biography of the composer with essays that go into greater detail on specific aspects of the composer's life.

GENRE SURVEYS

Lewis Lockwood surveys the symphonies in *Beethoven's Symphonies: An Artistic Vision* (New York: Norton, 2015), as does Martin Geck in *Beethoven's Symphonies: Nine Approaches to Art and Ideas* (Chicago: University of Chicago Press, 2017). Leon Plantinga provides a comparable overview in his *Beethoven's Concertos: History, Style, Performance* (New York: Norton, 1995). Charles Rosen introduces the piano sonatas in *Beethoven's Piano Sonatas: A Short Companion* (New Haven: Yale University Press, 2002), while Donald Francis Tovey's *A Companion to Beethoven's Pianoforte Sonatas*, first published in 1931 and now available in a revised edition by Barry Cooper, remains a classic (London: Associated Board of the Royal Schools of Music, 1998).

Joseph Kerman's *The Beethoven String Quartets* (New York: Norton, 1966), still the standard survey of the genre, is supplemented by a number of more recent publications, including *The Beethoven Quartet Companion*, ed. Robert Winter and Robert Martin (Berkeley: University of California Press, 1994); *The String Quartets of Beethoven*, ed. William Kinderman (Urbana and Chicago: University of Illinois Press, 2006); and Lewis Lockwood and the Juilliard String Quartet, *Inside Beethoven's Quartets: History, Interpretation, Performance* (Cambridge, MA: Harvard University Press, 2008).

Other genre surveys include *The Beethoven Violin Sonatas: History, Criticism, Performance*, ed. Lewis Lockwood and Mark Kroll (Urbana and Chicago: University of Illinois Press, 2004); Marc D. Moscovitz and R. Larry Todd, *Beethoven's Cello: Five Revolutionary Sonatas and Their World* (Woodbridge: Boydell Press, 2017); and Paul Reid, *The Beethoven Song Companion* (Manchester: Manchester University Press, 2007).

SPECIALIZED STUDIES

Robin Wallace examines the composer's deafness in *Hearing Beethoven: A Story of Musical Loss and Discovery* (Chicago: University of Chicago Press, 2018). Scott Burnham explores the musical basis for the perception of Beethoven's music as "heroic" in his *Beethoven Hero* (Princeton: Princeton University Press, 1995).

The composer's political views have been the focus of several recent studies, including Stephen Rumph's *Beethoven after Napoleon: Political Romanticism in the Late Works* (Berkeley: University of California Press, 2004); Nicholas Mathew's *Political Beethoven* (Cambridge: Cambridge University Press, 2013); and John Clubbe's *Beethoven: The Relentless Revolutionary* (New York: Norton, 2019).

The compositional process has long fascinated scholars, in part because the material is so rich: Beethoven himself preserved an enormous quantity of his sketches. Important studies include Barry Cooper, *Beethoven and the Creative Process* (Oxford: Clarendon Press, 1990); *Beethoven's Compositional Process*, ed. William Kinderman (Lincoln: University of Nebraska Press, 1991); and Lewis Lockwood, *Beethoven: Studies in the Creative Process* (Cambridge, MA: Harvard University Press, 1992). Douglas Johnson, Alan Tyson, and Robert Winter provide a detailed reconstruction and inventory of the sources in *The Beethoven Sketchbooks* (Berkeley: University of California Press, 1985). For a recent survey of the field, see Lewis Lockwood, "Beethoven's Sketches: The State of Our Knowledge." http://www.bu.edu/ beethovencenter/beethovens-sketches-the-state-of-our-knowledge/.

Performance issues are the focus of William S. Newman's *Beethoven on Beethoven: Playing His Piano Music His Way* (New York: Norton, 1988); *Performing Beethoven*, ed. Robin Stowell (Cambridge: Cambridge University Press, 1994); and Stewart Gordon's *Beethoven's 32 Piano Sonatas: A Handbook for Performers* (New York: Oxford University Press, 2016).

On the critical reception of the music, see Robin Wallace, *Beethoven's Critics: Aesthetic Dilemmas and Resolutions during the Composer's Lifetime* (Cambridge: Cambridge University Press, 1986); David B. Dennis, *Beethoven in German Politics, 1870–1989* (New Haven: Yale University Press, 1996); Esteban Buch, *Beethoven's Ninth: A Political History* (Chicago: University of Chicago Press, 2003); and Michael Broyles, *Beethoven in America* (Bloomington: Indiana University Press, 2011).

ONLINE RESOURCES

The Beethoven-Haus in Bonn maintains a museum housed in the composer's birth-house as well as an extensive archive of manuscript and printed sources, portions of which are available online: www.beethoven.de/en. The Ira F. Brilliant Beethoven Center at San Jose State University also houses a museum and archive as well as an excellent website with extensive bibliographies of both general and specialized topics related to the composer: www.sjsu. edu/beethoven/. Boston University's Center for Beethoven Research hosts regular conferences and concerts and maintains a valuable website of particular interest to scholars: www.bu.edu/beethovencenter/.

INDEX

Bold numerals indicate illustrations.

Razumofsky, Count Andrey Kirillovich (1752–1836), 57, 98
Rehding, Alexander, 130n.6, 131n.13
Reicha, Anton (1770–1836), 22
Reichardt, Johann Friedrich (1752–1814), 53, 55
rhetoric, 17
rhythm, 10, 25, 72, 95
Ries, Ferdinand (1784–1838), 25, 44, 45, 48, 55–56, 66, 90
Rochberg, George (1918–2005), 98
Rochlitz, Friedrich (1769–1842), 129n.1
Romberg, Andreas Jakob (1767–1821), 22
Romberg, Bernhard Heinrich (1767–1841), 22
rondo (form), 74, 93
Ronge, Julia, 121n.5, 127n.12
Roßner-Richarz, Maria, 126n.3
Royal Philharmonic Society, 6
Rudolph Johann Joseph Rainer, Archduke of Austria (1788–1831), 17, 27, 54, 56–57, 65, 66, 96, 97, 100
Russell, John (fl. 1824), 25–26

Sailer, Johann Michael (1751–1832), 33
Salieri, Antonio (1750–1825), 72, 115
  Falstaff, 126n.12
Saturday Night Fever (film), 112
Schaden, Joseph Wilhelm von (1754–1813), 124n.11
Schaller, Johann Nepomuk (1777–1842), 6
scherzo (genre), 75, 84, 93
Schiller, Friedrich (1759–1805), 31, 100, 109

Schindler, Anton (1795–1864), 20, 43, 48, 64, 90, 104, 105, 121n.7
Schlegel, Friedrich von (1772–1829), 8, 16
Schlosser, Johann Aloys (b. ca. 1790), 20
Schmidt, Julian (1818–1886), 7–8
Schoenberg, Arnold (1874–1951), 98
Schott (B.) Söhne (publisher), 28, 32
Schubert, Franz (1797–1828), 97
Schumann, Robert (1810–1856).
  Carnaval, op. 9, 104
self (concept), 30–31
Seyfried, Ignaz, Ritter von (1776–1841), 24, 124n.8
Shakespeare, William (1564–1616), 8, 31
  Romeo and Juliet, 91
  The Tempest, 90
Simrock, Nikolaus (1751–1832), 22, 64
Sisman, Elaine, 124n.12
Smetana, Bedřich (1824–1884).
  String quartet no. 1 ("From My Life"), 104–5
Smithson, Harriet Constance (1800–1854), 104
Solomon, Maynard, 109, 121n.2, 122n.4, 123n.3, 123n.12, 123n.13, 123n.14, 123n.15, 124n.2, 125n.3, 127n.7, 128n.1
sonata (form & genre), 58, 65–66, 68, 74, 75–77, 82, 89, 93
song (genre), 58, 68, 71, 88, 99
song cycle (genre), 48, 100
Sonnleithner, Joseph Ferdinand (1766–1835), 66
Spain, 66–67